NATURE
SPIRITUALITY
from the ground up

About the Author

Lupa is a Pagan author, artist, amateur naturalist, and wannabe polymath in Portland, Oregon. She is the author of several books on totemism and nature spirituality, and is the creater of the Tarot of Bones (summer 2016). She creates costuming, ritual tools, and other sacred art from hides, bones, and other natural materials. She is also a leading figure in the Vulture Culture. The organizer of Portland's Curious Gallery, a two-day art festival held annualy, it celebrates cabinets of curiosity and their contents. Lupa draws deeply from many wells of inspiration, from her Master's degree in counseling psychology and certification in ecopsychology to her many adventures in the forests, deserts, and coastal regions of Oregon. More about Lupa can be found at TheGreenWolf.com.

NATURE
SPIRITUALITY
from the Ground Up

Connect with Totems
in Your Ecosystem

LUPA

Llewellyn Publications
Woodbury, Minnesota

FIRST EDITION
First Printing, 2016

Cover design: Kevin R. Brown
Cover image: iStockphoto.com/11440578/©Chris Gramly
Editing: Laura Graves

Llewellyn Publications is a registered trademark of Llewellyn Worldwide Ltd.

Library of Congress Cataloging-in-Publication Data
Names: Lupa.
Title: Nature spirituality from the ground up : connect with totems in your
  ecosystem / Lupa.
Description: First Edition. | Woodbury : Llewellyn Worldwide, Ltd, 2016. |
  Includes bibliographical references and index.
Identifiers: LCCN 2015037458 | ISBN 9780738747828
Subjects: LCSH: Nature—Miscellanea. | Nature—Religious aspects.
  | Nature worship. | Totems—Miscellanea. | Spiritual life.
Classification: LCC BF1623.N35 L87 2016 | DDC 299/.94—dc23 LC record
available at http://lccn.loc.gov/2015037458

Llewellyn Publications
A Division of Llewellyn Worldwide Ltd.
2143 Wooddale Drive
Woodbury, MN 55125-2989
www.llewellyn.com

Printed in the United States of America

Other books by Lupa

Fang and Fur, Blood and Bone:
A Primal Guide to Animal Magic
(Megalithica Books, 2006)

DIY Totemism: Your Personal Guide to Animal Totems
(Megalithica Books, 2008)

Talking About the Elephant: An Anthology of
Neopagan Perspectives on Cultural Appropriation
(editor, Megalithica Books, 2009)

Skin Spirits: The Spiritual and Magical
Use of Animal Parts
(Megalithica Books, 2010)

New Paths to Animal Totems: Three Alternative Approaches to
Creating Your Own Totemism
(Llewellyn, 2012)

Engaging the Spirit World: Shamanism,
Totemism, and Animism
(editor, Megalithica Books, 2013)

Plant and Fungus Totems: Connect with Spirits
of Field, Forest, and Garden
(Llewellyn Worldwide, 2014)

Disclaimer

Throughout this book I will be recommending exercises that involve the reader going into the Great Outdoors, to include (if you're so inclined) wilderness areas. You are strongly advised to take reasonable precautions when going into such areas. Be aware of hazards such as inclement weather, wild animals, rash-causing plants, falling tree limbs, and the power of gravity combined with cliffs and other vertical drop-offs; while they may be beautiful and amazing parts of nature in and of themselves, under certain circumstances they can cause you illness, injury, or death. By all means, go outside and enjoy the world—just don't let your spirituality override common sense.

Also, while spiritual work can be incredibly fulfilling, it is not meant as a substitute for professional physical or mental health care, though it can be a good complement in some cases. Please do not stop taking medications or cease other treatment without consulting your health care professional(s).

The author, publisher, and all other related entities are not responsible for any injury, harm, death, property damage, or other adverse occurrences perpetrated by people using material from this book.

Contents

Introduction

Every day, I wake up. I take a deep breath of air and oxygen floods my system, just as it has with every other breath since the moment I entered this world. I stretch, and I listen. Sometimes I hear rain on the window. Sometimes I'm greeted by the songs of birds. Or I may wake to the voices of my neighbors in the driveway below. If I look out the window, I get to see the rain and the birds and the humans who share this patch of urban land.

I climb out of bed and seek out something for breakfast. Usually it's something simple like a bowl of cereal in milk. Occasionally I splurge and make eggs and bacon. Over the next few hours my body converts what I eat into energy, fueling my day of art or writing or errands or whatever else happens to be on tap.

And every one of these acts, no matter how ordinary, is at the same time sacred. That which is sacred inspires reverence and awe in the beholder; it helps them to feel closer to something greater than themselves. For some, that means a deity of some sort. To others, that "something greater" is the entirety of humanity.

For me, the sacred is nature—all of nature, not just the wildest parts. All of what I engage with in those first moments of my waking day, from the air and rain to the food and art, came in some way from a natural source. I include humans and our creations in "nature," too, for reasons I'll discuss later on in more detail. What's important to know now is that even living in the middle of a city, I spend every moment immersed in nature.

This is a book about nature spirituality. More specifically, it's a book on spirituality as a means to reconnect with nature. Those of us who live in more urban, industrialized settings often feel we are separate from nature, that we have changed our environments so much that we no longer deserve to be part of that community. We couldn't be further from the truth. In fact, if we are to reverse the damage we have done as a species, part of our task is to work on rebuilding connections to the rest of the world.

One way to do this is through working with totems, the overarching spiritual representatives of animals, plants, fungi, and other beings of nature who can act as intermediaries between us and the rest of nature. Animal totems are a common topic in spiritual writing, but they are usually presented on their own with little mention of the rest of their plant and fungus counterparts and the rest of what I call the totemic ecosystem, the vast spiritual network that mirrors physical ecosystems on our planet. I sometimes call this animals-only presentation "working with disembodied animals floating over our heads." In other words, the animal totems have no context or home; they're seen simply as beings that existed somewhere "out there in the spirit realms." Initially, my own practice was like this. What changed everything for me was moving to a place where the land itself embraced me and invited me to explore it in more detail, from the ground up. I found myself with more meaning and purpose for the spiritual practices I'd been working with for years as well as a deeper relationship to the land I lived with, and thus *bioregional totemism* was born. This type of spiritual practices is of course based on two particular concepts: totems and bioregions.

Totems, in my experience, are archetypal beings embodying all the qualities of a given species of animal, plant, or fungus, among other beings of nature; they are not simply individual spirits but sort of the deity or great guardian of their given species/groups. A totem is made of the natural history and behavior of its physical counterparts along with the relationships that species has with other beings (to include humans), as well as the lore and mythos we've built up around that type of fungus, plant, animal or other being. So when I work with Gray Wolf, I'm calling upon the behaviors, experiences, and lives of all gray wolves that have ever existed; the relationships wolves have with each other, their prey, and their environment; all the stories that we've told about wolves from Little Red Riding Hood to *White Fang* to *The Howling*; and my personal relationship with wolves. Chapter 3 will offer some information and context on what the various sorts of totems are, including some you may not have considered.

A **bioregion**, also known as an ecoregion, is a particular natural area defined by its physical and environmental components, such as the animals, plants, and fungi that live there, the geology and geography that shape the landforms, the waterways, the weather and climate, and so on. A bioregion may also be defined by the watershed of a major river; that is, all the land where water from precipitation drains into that river through creeks and streams. Chapter 2 deals with how to identify and connect with your bioregion, as well as how to find out what sorts of beings reside there.

This book is not about attaching generic meanings to animals, plants, and others in your local landscape; I'm not going to tell you how Wolf is the teacher and Corn is the mother and so on. Instead think of this as a guide to reconnecting with the greater community of nature, where you can make your own relationships with other beings and create personal connections together. You will not find a totem meaning dictionary in this book; if you still wish to have such a resource, please check Appendix A for recommended reading.

It is also not a book of "Native American totemism." My genetic background hails from assorted western and central European countries, but culturally I'm a Neopagan from the rural Midwest now residing in Portland, Oregon. I am an amateur naturalist and I love the outdoors and the place I live, from the basalt cliffs of the Columbia River Gorge to the rain that falls on the streets of Portland in winter. I dance with scrub jays and mule deer and little brown ants, morel mushrooms and broad-leaf maple trees and sword ferns. These things have more to do with what I write here than any indigenous American or European culture.

And it's meant not just for those who dwell in the wilderness, constantly surrounded by forests and deserts and prairies but also those of us who are more urban. A city is still a part of its bioregion. It may have changed the land quite a bit and shifted its inhabitants around some, but it is still reliant on local resources. I have worked with such totems as Redwood Tree, American Elk, and Paramecium, all in the comforts of a Portland apartment. No matter where you live, this book is still meant for you.

And it *is* about where you live. While it's certainly possible to work with the totems of beings halfway around the world, bioregional totemism particularly emphasizes establishing relationships with your local land and its inhabitants. We take our homes for granted all too often; when we become more aware of these vital places, we not only appreciate what they offer but we also become more invested in protecting them. I work with Redwood as a bioregional totem in part because there's a big redwood tree in the park near where I live and a few more scattered throughout the metro region; while they aren't native, they have made themselves pretty comfortable here. The totem Redwood reminds me of lessons learned in redwood forests further south in California, and together with that lone redwood in the park, helps me adjust to a landscape to which I am not native.

For those who travel, bioregional totemism offers a way to get more out of your trips. When I go out of town, I try to get at least one good hike or other outdoor experience wherever I go. Even if I am only in a park or on a trail for a couple of hours, I can use some of the exercises in this book to have a more meaningful encounter with my temporary home. It's good for helping me ground after hours or days of driving or crowded airplanes and trains, and it makes my excursion become more than simply going to a place and completing an itinerary. Just as I've made plenty of human friends in my travels, I've made totemic connections as well.

Because this is a self-and-spirit-created path, it's a constant work in progress; there's no holy writ that must be followed. You're welcome to adapt the material in this book (and my other writings, for that matter) to your own purposes and needs. I do recommend reading the book cover to cover first, just to get the full picture of what I'm presenting. After that, take what's most useful and modify or leave the rest as you will. You may also wish to keep a journal as you go through to take notes and record the results of any exercises and practices you try out. Additionally, it's always nice to be able to go back and see your progress over time.

The first few chapters lay the groundwork for the later material. Chapter 1 explores why we need to connect with nature, and what the benefits are of this reconnection. Chapter 2 is an introduction to bioregions, what they are and how to "meet" yours. In chapter 3, I discuss different types of totems you might meet, and in chapter 4 I'll get into how they form their own spiritual ecosystem, and how you can meet them there. Chapter 5 includes more meditation, rituals, and other practices to deepen your bond with the totems you meet. In chapter 6, I offer you a variety of ways to integrate your totemic spirituality into your everyday life.

The four appendices offer further resources to help you on your path. I want to mention Appendix D in particular. Please be aware that I rely quite a bit on guided meditation in this book. If you aren't very experienced with this practice or if you have trouble with it, Appendix D is a quick guide to trying it out and getting better at it.

A note on formatting: Throughout this book I will be referring to both individual species/categories, and the totems that watch over them. When I am speaking of the totems in specific, I capitalize the first letters of their names, so for example the totem of all red foxes is Red Fox, while the totem of all quartzite stones is Quartzite. On the other hand, the totem for the bird Cooper's hawk would be Cooper's Hawk; same thing with Bachman's warblers and their totem Bachman's Warbler. Additionally, some beings, particularly a number of plants and fungi, are known in the United States primarily by their Latin names. When I am speaking of the bacterium *Staphylococcus aureus*, note that I italicize the name (I may also shorten it to *S. aureus*). These conventions are taken from binomial nomenclature, the scientific system used to organize, classify, and name living beings. However, if I am writing about *S. aureus*'s totem, I will write it as Staphylococcus Aureus. (We totemists can be a little more informal.) I may sometimes refer to the physical beings as the totems' "physical counterparts" or their "children."

Also included are the terms "nature" and "nonhuman nature." Very often people think of "nature" as being anything that isn't humanity or its creations. However, for the purposes of this book, think of nature as including us—and yes, that includes our cities and technology and other uniquely human quirks. I mentioned that one of this book's predominant themes is remembering that we are a part of nature and reminding ourselves of that through our choice of language and definition. On the occasions when I need to refer to nature that doesn't include us, I'll use the term "nonhuman nature."

If you enjoy what you read, you may wish to take a look at my earlier books, *New Paths to Animal Totems* and *Plant and Fungus Totems*. In those works are some additional exercises in the bioregional chapters not found here, including a more thorough overview of animal, plant, and fungus totems.

Finally, you are always welcome to contact me with any questions or thoughts you have about what I've written. My email address is lupa.greenwolf@gmail.com and I can also be found on Facebook at http://www.facebook.com/TheGreenWolfLupa. And if you just can't get enough of my writings, check out my blogs at http://www.thegreenwolf.com/blog.com and www.patheos.com/blogs/pathsthroughtheforests/. My primary website and the portal for most things Lupa is ww.thegreenwolf.com, and information on my big art and writing project, The Tarot of Bones, may be found at www.thetarotofbones.com.

One

The Importance of
Reconnecting with Nature

My first "official" experience with Paganism and nature spirituality was facilitated by the moon. It was 1996, and I was seventeen years old and riding around the back roads of rural Missouri with some new friends of mine. As we drove along, I remarked on how beautiful the full moon was that night. This started a discussion about the mystical properties of Mama Luna, and I found myself amazed that there were other people who felt there was more to nature than scenery and resources.

But I'd felt that way since I was very young. I spent many long days throughout the year exploring the yards and open fields around each of my childhood homes, and I enjoyed a fascination with the outdoors that started from a very young age. Most of my positive childhood memories came from long summers spent digging in the moss and overturning rocks to see what was underneath; spring daffodils and periwinkles and the maple leaves that I played in and raked in autumn. I even still feel deep love for the cold Midwest winters when I would bundle up in many warm layers and spend hours in the snow, especially that first tangy taste of snowflakes on my tongue. Everything was wondrous and new, even if I'd seen it a hundred times before. The juniper bushes in the front yard, the rabbits that ran before me in the woods, the creek that sheltered minnows and crawdads—I never got tired of them, and they never ceased to greet me when I left the house each day.

My peers did not have the same love of nature, even though we all grew up in the same small town and surrounding region. No one in my immediate family was particularly interested in sharing my adventures either, and I was fairly isolated geographically and socially, so I didn't have much opportunity to get fresh perspectives from elsewhere. Finding my first group of Pagan peers was a crucial moment in my life. Finding other people who believed the land was sacred was like arriving ashore after years of being alone and adrift at sea.

Discovering Paganism was just the first step in my realization that I wasn't alone. Over time I discovered a variety of people, from environmentalists to avid hikers to hunters to ecotherapists, who appreciated and connected to nature. But I found we were still the minority. Most people I ran into in the US weren't all that concerned about the nonhuman inhabitants of this world. Fewer still saw themselves as part of nature, and even among nature-lovers was a strong perceived disconnection between humans and everything else. We were supposed to only preserve nature that didn't have humans in it or remove the humans from nature to protect it. A few even went so far as to describe us as "parasites" or "a cancer on the earth." I beg to differ. While humans are definitely an incredibly destructive species, we're also quite a creative one as well. And I believe there are much more constructive and life-affirming solutions to the current environmental crisis than telling people "You don't deserve to be here. Why don't you just die?" or to sink into a wallow of despairing inactivity until we really do all pass away.

There are no easy solutions, and the ones we've come up with either aren't always effective, or aren't implemented as widely as they should be. However, I believe our ambivalence and lack of motivation are due in part to one very nasty force—disconnection.

Why Reconnect?

The older I get and the more I perceive and experience and learn, the more I believe a sense of disconnection is what's at the heart of so many environmental (and social, economic, and other) problems today. Let's look at disconnection from nonhuman nature in particular. Ancestral humans—and some people still today—became intimately entwined with their land not only as individuals but as cultures. They learned everything they could about the animals, plants, and fungi living alongside them, and they knew the weather patterns and seasons, the ways the land was shaped, as well as where the special and sacred places were. The land was not dead nor only meant for the taking; it was full of a vibrant array of neighbors of many types, some of whom became good friends and allies. We needed each other to survive; humans evolved as a social species that hunted and foraged together, slept together, protected each other, and helped each other raise the younger members of the group to adulthood. We had to consciously rely on an intricate interconnection with many beings and phenomena.

This is a much less common experience today. We take for granted that we'll have access to food, shelter, and other resources, and rarely have to think about where these things come from. We don't need to get to know a particular patch of land in depth beyond knowing where the nearest bank, grocery store, and employment opportunities are. Fewer and fewer of us live in the places we were born in or even grew up in (I myself was an Army brat born in Frankfurt am Main, Germany, but grew up in the Midwest of the US). When we don't feel connected to a place, it becomes anonymous, and that anonymity is what allows us to be so destructive: we believe we don't have to care about something we know nothing about. We depersonalize the land and then simply take what we want from it, thinking there won't be any consequences. But when we do this, we're actually destroying our own life-support system.

Some of the need for reconnection is physically practical. But it's also emotional and psychological. We spent millions of years evolving in wild places—first the African savannah, and then later throughout other parts of the world. We cannot undo our brains' hard-wiring toward nature so easily. When we feel disconnected from the rest of the world, it takes a toll on our psychological health, as well as our sense of security in belonging to a more-than-human community. Theodore Roszak, one of the original ecopsychologists, states that "In devastating the natural environment, we may be undermining a basic requirements of sanity: our sense of moral reciprocity with the non-human environment" (Roszak, 2012). Being so self-centered breeds a sad loneliness in us as individuals and as a species.

We are not without hope or resources, however. Recent studies have demonstrated the basic positive response humans have to nature and offer more evidence to support, as Roszak continues, "taking our evolutionary heritage seriously and putting it in an ecological framework." In 2008, researchers compared the stress relieving effects of a window facing a natural scene, a plasma screen with a live feed of the same scene, and a blank wall. People who were able to look out the window had the best results; those who faced the plasma screen, even with its nature scene, did no better than those facing the blank wall. Our minds are not fooled by our technology.

That study is just one of many demonstrating what Richard Louv says in *The Nature Principle*: "the long-held belief that nature has a direct positive impact on human health is making the transition from theory to evidence and from evidence to action" (46). He follows this up with citations of studies promoting nature as an antidote to everything from heart disease to dementia, pain to mood disorders. Science is catching up with the long-known concept that nature is good for us.

Part of nature's positive effects can be chalked up to what's known as "soft fascination." When we're walking in a largely human-dominated environment, be it a city or town or even a lake with a lot of boaters, we're forced to focus on many immediate, attention-grabbing stimuli and distractions at once. Where are the other people around us, how far away are they, what sort of noise are they making, and do I need to interact with any of them? Where am I going, and have I gotten lost? What sorts of background noises am I contending with, and how am I having to navigate traffic, either on foot or in a vehicle? Am I on time? Am I in a hurry? How do my eyes meet all the hard, harsh lines of the buildings, and how do I tune out all the advertisements on billboards, signs, newspapers, buses, radios? Do I have enough money to complete the task ahead of me, and do I need to coordinate with other people to make this happen? What's that sudden sound, and is that car going to stop before I step into the crosswalk? And where did I park *my* car anyway (and has the meter run out)?

Soft fascination, by contrast, allows our minds to drift organically and smoothly from stimulus to thought to observation. Unless we are suddenly startled by an animal stomping through the woods or a tree branch falling or some other potentially dangerous thing, we can gently pay attention to what's going on around us without having to constantly deal with a barrage of stimuli. Our focus isn't grasped and pulled to and fro by sights, sounds, and startlements, but instead is allowed to wander as it will. As outlined by the researchers who coined the term, "Soft fascination may be a mixture of fascination and pleasure such that any lack of clarity an individual may be experiencing is not necessarily blotted out by distraction, but rendered substantially less painful" (Kaplan and Kaplan, 192).

There are also social and community-based benefits to re-connecting with nonhuman nature. When we feel connected to someone or something, we feel more of a sense of responsibility toward it. Remember that part of the reason so many people seem to blithely ignore the effect their choices have on the rest of the world human and otherwise is due to the anonymity of those who are affected. As a general rule, we're less likely to have compassion for someone or something we don't know. By creating more personal connections with our bioregion and its inhabitants, we lessen that anonymity. Better yet, we can transfer that compassion to other locations; after all, if our own special places suffer from pollution and other destruction, then surely so must others. This makes us more likely to feel responsible for nature all over the planet, not just our own backyards.

When we lessen the degree of anonymity, we become free to believe that it's okay to have a sense of responsibility without being overwhelmed by guilt. Many people feel very helpless in the face of our many environmental problems such that they choose not to act. It's not that these people are uncaring; they may think there's nothing they can do (hopelessness) or that they don't deserve to be environmentalists (fear of hypocrisy). Or they may be turned off by the occasional hyperaggressive and hypercritical methods more radical activists use, usually guilt and shaming tactics. As a result, many people choose to distance themselves from anything that reminds them of the current ecological crisis, even going so far as to deny humanity a place in nature; an effort to protect the environment as well as their own sense of well-being. Richard Nelson puts it poignantly:

> *It's dangerous to think of ourselves as loathsome creatures or as perversions in the natural world. We need to see ourselves as having a rightful place. We take pictures of all kinds of natural scenes and often we try to avoid having a human being in them ... In our society, we force ourselves into a greater and greater distance from the natural world by creating parks and wilderness areas where our only role is to go in and look. And we call this loving it.* **We lavish tremendous concern and care on scenery but we ignore the ravaging of environments from which our lives are drawn** *(Nelson in Gardner, 1998). (Emphasis mine.)*

The truth is, we never actually left the community of nature; we just think and act as though we did. Through this attitude we justify some of our species' most destructive behaviors. By rejoining that community not as destroyers or plagues but as one part of a vibrant family, we empower ourselves and others to be more active in its protection.

When we remember that humans are a part of nature, we also can extend our increased compassion and regard to members of our own species. A stronger, healthier community of human beings is more capable of facing the challenges of environmental destruction and imbalance. It's not that people who are poor or oppressed just don't care about the environment; however, when each day is mostly taken up with scrabbling to survive in a hostile environment, self-preservation is usually a lot more of immediate concern than environmental preservation. Sometimes that choice of self over all else affects the land directly; as one example, a lot of poaching of endangered species is done by people who sell the animals because they have few options for income, or by people who simply eat what they've killed because there's no other food available. There are certainly cases of disadvantaged communities engaged in environmental activism both for their own benefit and that of the land itself, but it would be even easier for them to accomplish their goals if they were less stressed by hunger, poverty, racism, and other significant problems. Impoverished places are more likely to be the site of toxic pollution, illegal logging and/or mining, and other environmental ills because the perpetrators think the people there can't fight back; an empowered community is more able to fight back against these injustices. It behooves would-be environmentalists to also be aware of and involved in more specifically human issues both for their own sake and the environmental benefits of healthy human communities.

Healing the Rift Between Spiritual and Physical

In my first years as a Pagan, I participated in a more subtle form of disconnection from nature. Deprived of the small, wild places I'd grown up with (which had been bulldozed by developers wanting to build more ticky-tacky boxes), and then living in a particularly urban area of Pittsburgh with few green spaces and lots of pavement, I did what many Pagans do: I latched on to the abstract symbols and projections of nature in the forms of gods, totems, spirits, and the like. The first goddess to call on me was Artemis, keeper of the hunt and wildlife, and over time I worked with other deities and spirits who represented or were otherwise connected to natural phenomena.

Now, there's nothing wrong with only focusing one's practice on the gods and spirits and such. Some people wouldn't characterize their beliefs as being nature-based, even when worshipping deities strongly associated with natural phenomena, but instead root their paths in ancient cultures and their values. They also may see the gods and spirits as self-contained independent beings that do not embody natural forces. However, if a person is going to practice what they claim is a specifically *nature*-based path, it's important to not mistake the map for the territory.

What do I mean by that? Well, let's look at totems as an example. They are not themselves the physical animals, plants, and other beings inhabiting the dirt-and-flesh world. They are nonphysical beings that hold the qualities of their given species. Bald Eagle is "made of" the natural history and behavior of bald eagles as well as the mythology and folklore about bald eagles. Those myths and tales are based heavily on human observation of the physical animal itself. If you only look at the abstract and symbolic qualities of a being that is so deeply connected to its physical counterparts, you're missing its entire foundation. Why is the eagle often seen as a messenger from the divine? We can guess that at least part of it is the fact that eagles are able to soar to quite great heights, and we could imagine they might even be able to go up to where the gods reside in the sky. (Most people also think eagles are much prettier than their similarly high-flying neighbors, vultures and condors, which helps to turn eagles into a more romantic myth.) In short, to understand natural spirituality more deeply, it's necessary to know the natural history that feeds it.

It is possible to be spiritual and only engage with the physical world, bypassing totems and other beings entirely. If I walk into the wilderness and meet up with a coyote, not much is going to happen if I try talking to that coyote; it's not going to impart great wisdom to me in English. What I can gain, however, are insights and a measure of relaxation simply by observing the coyote in the wilderness, which is a wonder in and of itself. I can even think like a coyote a bit, and adopt some of what I see the coyote do into my own behavior. Some people are content limiting their spirituality to these moments of joy and quiet observation in the physical world. Others also value the structure of mythology and ritual, and the beings that populate these stories and practices. They ask the totems to tell them more about that coyote, or that sugar pine, or that basalt outcropping.

Totems and their ilk are capable of communicating with us in ways their physical counterparts can't and in doing so can help us understand and appreciate all of nature even more deeply than before. We can draw on the myths and lore surrounding the totems and use them to create rituals rooted in meaning, connection, and the celebration of nature.

Bioregional totemism, then, is a blending of these things. It is the moments of awe and wonder we can have in experiences with physical nature itself—the catch of breath at the sight of a raptor taking flight, or the fragile beauty of fog from the exhalations of plants in a glass terrarium. It's also a structure for creating more personal meaning for these things, meanings that add to rather than replace their inherent physical qualities. It's a reminder that there is magic in ritual and practice, and the physical world has magic to offer, too, embodied in wonder and awe. It is a path that draws on both the map and the territory.

In this way, this book and some of my others are intentionally subversive. Some people come to Paganism and similar paths because they want magic in their lives and don't see it in the everyday world. They want to learn spells and rituals and work with spiritual beings but they want to do so as an escape from the "mundane" physical reality, or because somewhere along the line they lost touch with physical nature just as I did, focusing strongly on the symbols of what they lost. What I love seeing is when someone who starts with the trappings and mystique eventually works their way into the roots and fertile dirt beneath the shiny surface. Animal totems lead to animals, which lead to care for the animals' habitats and the plants and fungi and waters and others, bringing together the allure of the mystical and the communion with the physical.

From Point A to Point B

So how do we make all this reconnection happen? It's not a simple process, especially on a community-wide level. The best place to start is yourself, and I'd like to offer a few practices to help you on your way.

Collecting the Sacred and the Valued

One of the things I love about spiritual exploration is that it's an opportunity to be more aware of what you consider to be important and special. This exercise is designed to help you identify some of your values and other sacred things (in this context "sacred" doesn't have to be purely religious or spiritual).

First, get paper and a pen or open a document file on your computer. Make two columns. At the top of one write "What are my values?" and at the top of the other "What is sacred to me?" Then list as many things under each heading as you like. I recommend giving yourself at least ten minutes for each column; you can do one and then the other or bounce back and forth as you feel inspired.

For the values column, focus on personal qualities, behaviors, and beliefs you think are important to embody or otherwise believe are essential for your life. You can also identify cultural values—the qualities, behaviors, and beliefs considered to be important in the cultures, communities, or families of which you are a part. Some examples of values include frugality, independence, playfulness, compassion, accomplishment, and patience, among many others. If you get stuck or need some inspiration, there's a great list of values at humanityquest.com/.

What you consider "sacred" is generally (though not exclusively) going to refer to beings, places, and things in the world you inhabit, rather than within you, that you consider particularly deserving of great care, reverence, and respect. You can be very general about this, such as "nature" or "life," or get into more specifics like "the field I use for spiritual celebrations," "the times when the rain falls while the sun is shining," or "the white deer I see on occasion when I am hiking." It can also refer to practices such as prayers, meditations, or rituals done to honor these things.

This can be a challenging exercise, especially if you've never consciously identified and quantified your values and sacred concepts before. (I sometimes think of them as being similar to art; I may not be able to put into words what *makes* something art to me, but I know it when I see it.) You may also find that you identify values and sacred things you hadn't even realized were important to you or ones that you want to incorporate into your life more.

Next, identify your top ten values and top ten sacred things. Then narrow it down to five of each, and then your top three. Narrowing your list doesn't mean the ones you didn't pick aren't important, and it can be tough to choose. But knowing which ones are especially important can help you better understand where your personal priorities are.

Why go through all this trouble when you very well may already feel that nature is important to you? Isn't that what this is all about? Well yes, chances are that if you're reading this book nature is something near and dear to you. But connection can happen on a variety of levels and for many reasons. I can share "nature" as a sacred concept (or value) with ten people, but we may feel differently about related values such as conservation, cooperation, money, and spirituality. These differences can make our personal relationships with nature unique... and sometimes in conflict with each other. However, if we can also find other values we share with other people, they can help us to bridge the gaps between the things we may not always agree on.

Even if you're looking at your values and sacred things for your own benefit, it's one thing to be able to say "I feel nature is important and sacred," and another thing entirely to be able to explain more fully why you feel that way. The first time I did this exercise, my top three values were independence, nature, and creativity. Through introspection, I found that I valued nature in part because it is a system composed of a variety of types of beings, each with its own qualities and behaviors, thus independent from all others in many ways. The diversity of nature, then, inspires me to value my own independence and that of others (though I also, in turn, value the *inter*dependence in nature as well). As to creativity, the many and varied forms that nature takes—from animals to stones to weather patterns—are an inspiration to me as an artist, and they bring forth in me a deep wonder at the world I am fortunate enough to be part of. Knowing the reasons behind my values gives me more of a sense of purpose and energy to keep creating and exploring.

You can revisit your values and sacred things periodically as you continue in your spiritual journeys. It's a good way to reassess the direction your path is going and the reasons you're walking it. If you decide to collaborate with other people spiritually or otherwise, you can use this exercise to be aware of things you may share with them, as well as areas to build bridges across differences (or just leave them be, if that's the better option).

———

Sadie is just getting started on her spiritual path; she grew up in a largely nontheistic household where spirituality was simply not a topic of conversation or practice. However, her family's love of outdoor activities like camping and boating helped her become interested in nature spirituality. She wants to proceed carefully and with better self-awareness, so she makes a list of her values and concepts she considers sacred, worthy of protection and upholding. In doing so, she finds that some of her most important values are community, activity, and learning, and she considers her local watershed and her family and friends to be sacred to her. Through a friend she finds out about a nonprofit group that works to protect the watershed, and she invites some of her family to go to a meeting with her. She and her sister really like it and become active members; their relationship becomes even stronger as they work together for a common purpose. While the nonprofit group isn't particularly spiritual, Sadie does find a lot of inspiration out in the wetlands and estuaries she helps to clean up and protect, and she feels closer to the other volunteers out there with her. She believes that perhaps the love she is developing for these places and the care she has for the people who share similar feelings could be the start of something much deeper and more meaningful to her.

———

Go Take a Hike!

This is a multi-purpose exercise. For our overall purposes, it's a good way to start noticing things about your home and surrounding area you may have taken for granted. It's especially useful if you don't normally walk around very much; when we walk through a place rather than drive or bike, we take in details more thoroughly and slowly. And when we aren't responsible for a vehicle and a specific route and destination, we're free to explore the place where we are right that moment with fewer distractions.

It's based in the soft fascination concept mentioned earlier, where your awareness drifts and moves more naturally and with much less stress. You might find that even after trying it just once, you're more aware of what's going on around you on a regular basis. The more you practice, the more it can help you to open your perception beyond whatever your immediate goal or destination may be and value the journey as much as the destination.

Keep in mind that in this exercise, "hike" is relative. What you'll be doing is carefully exploring your immediate area—your neighborhood, yard, tiny little town, farm, and so on. Even if you're confined indoors or to your bed, you can participate. If you need assistance, get someone you trust who is willing to explore with you.

Starting in your home, maybe even your bedroom (wherever you consider a good starting point), begin moving slowly and deliberately outward. Explore the boundaries of this room as though you have never been there before and need to describe it to someone else. Notice the colors and textures of the objects and decorations, any animals or plants, and what makes this room unique. Continue this exploration throughout the rest of your home.

Now, if you're willing and able, head outside. Observe from a window if you need to stay indoors for any reason. Be mindful of what's around you. Don't worry about knowing the names of all the animals or plants you encounter or having a particular destination. Just observe slowly and deliberately, moving as you see fit in the moment. Notice this yard, neighborhood, and street as though it is entirely new to you and you will need to take stories of it with you. Pay attention to the people you see too, as they're as much as part of this place as anything else. Do be careful if you're going into rough terrain, and keep yourself safe (don't walk into traffic, off a cliff, etc.).

Keep exploring your outdoor area. Stay where you feel comfortable, and don't worry about rushing along. Make note of what you feel as you're observing, but don't let feelings distract your observations—notice them and move on.

Every so often throughout this exercise, stop a moment. Identify five things you can see, five things you can hear, and five things you can touch. Don't worry about naming them; just observe them and continue. Repeat this part of the exercise periodically, especially if you find your thoughts or attention wandering from your exploration; it's a good way to reground yourself in the moment.

Once you're about ready to be done, head back home while continuing to simply observe. If possible, come home by a different route than the one on which you left. Go back inside, and complete the exercise by going to the place you started. Take a moment to breathe and be in that place. Then do something to bring you back to your normal state of mind.

Being more aware of where you are and who and what inhabits that place is a good start to reconnecting. We may have become disconnected in part because we lost track of our surroundings, shutting out everything and everyone around us except what seemed most immediately important. This exercise presents a simple way to start closing the perceived divide between us and everything else. After you've done this exercise a time or two, you may notice yourself being more aware of what's around you, even when you aren't actively trying. Certain things in your environment like a particular plant or landform might stand out more once you consciously notice them. Pay attention to those things that capture your attention; you may want to follow up with them in later exercises.

The other benefit of this exercise and others like it is that it's very grounding. When my anxiety starts to get really overwhelming, I'll sometimes do this exercise to distract myself from whatever's got me worried long enough to calm down and then go back and deal with the issue more rationally (if the issue hasn't just gone away on its own, that is). If I can't do the full exercise as described, like if I don't have enough time or can't leave the place I'm at, I'll use the part where I identify five things I can see, hear, and touch.

Feel free to adapt the exercise to your purposes; if you are not able to do a part of the exercise, don't worry about it. For example, if you're deaf, you may wish to cut the portion that involves noticing things you can hear (unless you want to identify things other people may hear, or things you used to be able to hear if you haven't always been deaf). If you live in a neighborhood that isn't very safe, stick to areas where you feel you'll be okay, and take someone along if you think it'll help. If the place you really want to connect to is down the street or a little further like a park or wooded area, go to that place as safely as you can and then begin the exercise.

Remembering Our Place in Nature

This exercise has two parts. As the title suggests, it is meant to help you be aware of being a human animal entwined with the bioregion you live in. It also demonstrates how much we have in common with other animals and helps us to reclaim our place among them rather than above them.

Part I—Guided Meditation

For this first part, you will be exploring how the various parts of your human body and mind are gifts from nature. No matter how urban you are, no matter if you've never spent a single night asleep under the open sky, you are still the product of millions upon millions of years of natural evolution. You can memorize this meditation (or the basic process of it, if not word-for word). Or you may wish to have someone read it for you, or record yourself reading it and then meditate along with the recording.

Get yourself into a safe place where you won't be disturbed for an hour or so. Turn off your phone and any other distractions, and do what you need to do make yourself comfortable. If you have a preferred pose for long meditations you can use that, or you may simply sit or lay down if you prefer.

Now, focus on your breathing for a moment or two. Feel how the air moves in through your nose, down your throat, deep into your lungs, causing your chest to gently expand, and then out again. Hold your breath for a count of five, and then inhale again, deeply. Feel how nice it is to fulfill your body's need for oxygen. Our lungs developed in far-back fish ancestors who needed more than just gills to pull in precious air as they began to explore dry land, and even today there is no substitute for life-giving oxygen or the lungs we use to draw it in. From these amphibian ancestors we have the ability to breathe as we do.

Next, move your attention to the muscles in your belly, back, and chest that help your lungs expand and contract. Feel how they connect to the muscles in your limbs and your neck and head, how you are covered in strong, red muscle. Flex your muscles, feel how they harden, and then let them relax. Even your heart is made of powerful muscles, beating thousands of times every day, and your tongue is made of strong muscles as well, without which you could not speak or eat as well as you do now. Our muscles were passed down to us from ancient generations of invertebrates well over five hundred million years ago. Their need to move along the ocean floor is echoed in every action we take, from walking down the street to shopping for food. We go from place to place because our long-ago ancestors made the first move with the innovation of muscles.

Bring your attention to the muscles that move your eyes. If you're comfortable, open your eyes gently and notice how you're able to detect light and shadow, color, shapes, movement, and depth in an instant. Hundreds of millions of years ago, some of the earliest and tiniest animals developed the ability to sense light, and over many generations this basic ability blossomed into complex eyes, not once but many times. One of these success stories led to the eyes of an aquatic ancestor, eyes which every vertebrate species since then has inherited.

Now, move your focus to your teeth and jaws and mouth, and then down your throat to your stomach and intestines and out of your body again. Think of the last thing you ate today, what you ate yesterday, and perhaps the day before. Think of the food in your fridge and pantry, and think of restaurants you like to go to and what you order there. Consider how your body can take all kinds of food, from meat to vegetables to grains, among others, more types of food than most other animals on this planet, and how you can convert those foods into the building blocks of your body and the energy you burn to live. The earliest organisms billions of years ago fed on sunlight, and later in time on each other; like them, we eat other living beings, animal, plant, and fungus, to go on living. Our jaws and teeth are a gift from some of the earliest fish, and the flora in our gut that help us to digest are descended from those that made a pact with our ancestors so very long ago. Even our most recent ancestors, humans and other hominid species, diverged from their fruit-eating forebears and used a diet including meat to become stronger, smarter, and even more successful. While we can choose from a variety of diets today, we owe our tastes to many different dining opportunities.

Move your attention to your skin and your hair. Sense how warm you are, how you create heat rather than just feeling it. Imagine your body is a furnace burning the food you eat to keep you just the right temperature. Each cell has a tiny fire in it burning via the process of metabolism. The earliest mammals developed ways to regulate their internal temperature. Later descendants fine-tuned being warm-blooded and developed hair to insulate and protect. We owe our warmth to these ancestors; without them our lives might be much chillier indeed.

Finally, bring your attention to your brain, the seat of your mind. Think of everything you are capable of, from moving your body around to making decisions, planning, learning, teaching, building, and playing. All these are behaviors and abilities our ancestors learned, from the most basic primitive unicellular response systems to the home-building skills of ants and birds and rodents and so many others, from the social skills of the ancestors of mammals to the careful patience of many predators lying in wait.

Consider for a moment that we are made of all of these and other gifts from our ancestors. We are not unnatural beings. Even our most seemingly artificial of creations are driven by basic needs—to eat nourishing food and drink clean water, to be safe and healthy and sheltered, to communicate and not be alone, to pass on genes and resources. We are the same as all the others, descended from a long line of innovative ancestors whose gifts to use survive to this day. Take a moment to feel gratitude for these gifts that you have here in the present.

When you are ready, slowly open your eyes and come back to the waking world. Stretch if you need to, slowly move around, and be back in your everyday mind.

———

Once you're done, eat something to ground yourself, and record any notes you may wish to make about your experiences. The sooner you record them the better, while they're still fresh in your mind. You can review your progress in your totemic work in later months and see how well the meditation stuck. You might even try doing this meditation periodically, perhaps a few times a year, to reaffirm your place in nature and see if you learn new things from the meditation each time.

———

Tomás has been in a wheelchair for four years, ever since he was badly injured in a car wreck. Before the accident, he had spent almost every weekend hiking, camping, kayaking, and being otherwise very active outdoors. Once he came home from the hospital, he fell into a deep depression due to feeling more limited in his options and the ongoing pain from his injuries. Over time, he reached out to other people who had been similarly paralyzed and discovered ways to still live a wonderfully fulfilling life. Still, his inability to hike on rougher trails left him feeling distanced from the nature he once enjoyed. One day while on his way down to a nearby grocery store, he slows down a bit and begins to notice the trees and other plants along the sidewalk. Some of them are similar to those he saw while hiking, but others he's never even noticed before. Then at the store he pays more attention to the plants in the produce section, and out of curiosity reads the labels that tell where they all come from; he's surprised to see how many are from thousands of miles away, while only a few are from his own state. For the next couple of weeks, every time he's out and about he notices more and more gardens in his neighborhood and wonders that with all the green growing things around him, why does so much food still comes from so far away? Tomás decides that he wants to find out more about local food production and joins an organization for urban farming and community gardens. With the help of a few of his friends, he's able to build some raised planting boxes and paved pathways in his yard (and gets those friends involved in the farming group as well). Some of the boxes he dedicates to food production, but he also saves a few corners for some of the plants he enjoyed on his hikes. His physical relationship to the outdoor world may have been changed some due to his injury, but he has reclaimed some of that joy and connection he developed before.

———

Part II—Daily Awareness

The second part of this exercise involves being mindful from moment to moment. Many people are unable to do in-depth meditations every day for any of a number of understandable reasons. Even if you have a very busy life you can still take a minute to reconnect and be aware of what you're doing and where you are. Here are a few instances where you can use a little mindfulness to keep that connection with nature alive:

- Whether it's a quick snack or a full meal, appreciate for a moment your complex digestive system while eating. Consider where your food came from, what animals, plants, and/or fungi you're eating. Think of the soil that supports them, the basis of their habitats. And consider how much water went into the preparation of what you're eating, as well as hydrating these beings while they were alive. When you take this moment of mindfulness, you might think to yourself "I am a child of nature. I eat and I drink like my ancestors before me, and I honor all those who have given of themselves to feed me."

- While drifting off to sleep, consider that this is an experience we share with all other mammals and many other creatures as well. No matter how much we may drug ourselves with stimulants and force ourselves to work long hours, eventually our bodies tell us "Stop. Rest. Recharge." As you prepare to sleep, you may think "I am a child of nature. I am about to give my mammalian body the rest it needs to recover from today and make the most of tomorrow."

- When going from a motionless state to an active one, such as standing up and beginning to walk, think of the very first animals to move around, ancient sea creatures that developed very basic locomotion to escape danger or find food. Think of how successful this ability to move has been, and be aware of your own ability to move from place to place, however that may be done. As you go from stillness to motion, think to yourself "I am a child of nature. For millions of years my ancestors have swum, rolled, flown, and run in the water, land, and air. Like them, I now move across the earth to get to where I need to go."

- If you hug someone you care for, snuggle with a partner, or otherwise find comfort in a gentle touch shared with another, consider also how many other animals, mammals and others, have taken solace in each other's physical presence. Think of how this instinct developed to help animals create stronger social bonds for survival, and how for many people touch conveys a sense of safety. If that's how you feel in this moment, enjoy it and appreciate it, and think "I am a child of nature. In kindness and contact I and other animals find joy and security, and like others I take this moment to appreciate good company."

- If you find yourself surrounded by buildings, or even just in your own home, think about how other animals create shelters. Most birds build nests, some mammals burrow in the ground, some insects create elaborate cities in the earth or in towers of dirt. We humans build shelters, too. They may be much more large and complex than even the biggest termite mound, but the urge to build comes from the same animal source. As you observe your surroundings think to yourself, "I am a child of nature. I seek shelter and a place to return to, a home to call my own. I am of a species that has specialized in ever-greater and varied structures, but in the end we all want the same thing: a place to be safe and sound."

You are of course welcome to create your own moments of mindfulness and awareness. What's important is that you find that connection to nature, and the things that remind you that you are a part of it, not a detached bystander.

———

By now I hope you've found some compelling reasons to reconnect with nature, nonhuman and human alike. In the next chapter we'll explore the place where you live in even more detail with the concept of bioregionalism before heading off to meet the totems themselves in chapter 3.

Two

The Basics of Bioregionalism

One of the beautiful things about totemism in a global society is that we're able to find out about and work with totems from around the world. Someone in Cleveland, Ohio, can ask Giant Baobab (whose physical counterparts reside in Madagascar) for help with learning to use resources more wisely. Meanwhile, a totemist in Brisbane, Queensland, Australia, might get a message in a dream from Common Cuckoo even though they've never been to Europe. And because so many of us have easy access to information about all sorts of beings in this world thanks to mass publishing and the Internet, we can find out more about these totems and their children once we've identified them.

There's also something to be said for keeping totemism closer to home. This isn't to promote any sort of xenophobia or other unsavory agenda; rather think of it as a more elaborate spiritual manifestation of the "bloom where you're planted" concept. By getting to know the totems of the beings that populate your locale, you can learn to connect even more deeply with that place. This can then foster a feeling of comfort and being at home. Just as you can meet human neighbors who live near you and even form friendships, you can do the same with nonhuman neighbors, too. (I'll explain more about why you may wish to nurture these bonds with totems in the next chapter.)

There are plenty of ways to identify your location. When someone asks you where you live, you probably give your town or city name. You might also mention your street address, or your state or province, depending on the situation. If you're traveling abroad there's a good chance you'll be asked to identify your country of origin. All of these are very human-centered ways of organizing places, and while there's nothing wrong with them in and of themselves, I'd like to focus on something that centers on nature as a whole (humans included): the bioregion.

Bioregions Defined

Also known as an ecoregion,[1] a bioregion is a place defined by common natural features, most often land forms and watersheds that determine what native flora and fauna can live there

---

1. There is some debate as to whether a bioregion denotes a larger area than an ecoregion; some people consider the watershed of the Mississippi River in the Midwestern United States to be a bioregion, covering large portions of several states and provinces, while the watersheds of smaller tributary rivers are considered ecoregions. For the purposes of this book I will be using the term bioregion in a more general manner, as is the common layperson's usage.

and that have a profound effect on the local climate. Within a particular bioregion, you would expect to find mostly the same animals, plants, and fungi; similar climate and weather; and geology with common features with some local variation of any and all of the above. You may find multiple types of ecosystems within the same bioregion; a bioregion in a temperate zone may have some areas that are forested, some that are grassy, and some wetlands. However, all the forests in that bioregion will generally have the same features, and the same goes for all the grasslands and all the wetlands.

Bioregions often overlap or lay within each other's boundaries. Here in Portland, Oregon, I live in the Portland Basin, a depression in the ground formed during the Miocene Epoch approximately twenty million years ago. While the Columbia River began to deposit sediment into the basin soon after and humans later filled it in even more, it's still recognizable as a geological formation today. It's not a bioregion in and of itself, but I consider it one of my most immediate nonhuman location markers.

I am also located where the Willamette River drains into the Columbia River. I am in a nest of bioregions; the portion of Portland I'm in has been drastically changed by human hands and its native species have mostly been depleted save some birds, small mammals and reptiles, and invertebrates. It's tucked within the Willamette's watershed, a region stretching hundreds of miles to the south of the city through fields and farmland. In fact, both the Environmental Protection Agency and the World Wildlife Fund agree that the "official" bioregion for this area is the Willamette Valley bioregion.

However, in my experience it is the Columbia River that is the main artery of this area, so I also consider its watershed to be an important bioregion. In fact, this is often considered to be the heart of the larger Cascadia bioregion, which encompasses a significant part of the Pacific Northwest United States and adjacent portions of Canada.

So if I were to give my "bioregional address," I might say that I live in the Portland Basin, Willamette Valley, Cascadia (or the Columbia River Watershed). Of course, the assumption is that whomever I was talking to would have a similar understanding of the local area. Additionally, other Portlanders might adopt other local landmarks to be their bioregional street address.[2] All this illustrates the basic concept of what a bioregion is, and you can find out more about your own at en.wikipedia.org/wiki /Lists_of_ecoregions_by_country.

Your Bioregional Address

Let's look at that address concept again for a moment. If you were going to describe your bioregional address to someone, what might it be? Whereas with street addresses we usually start with the house or apartment number and work outward, here it may be easier to start big and work your way in.

First, identify your ecoregion using the link in the last section or a similar resource (you can try contacting local con-

---

2. Later on in this book I'll be introducing a couple more specialized concepts related to bioregions, known as biomes and biotopes, which can enhance your understanding of your bioregional address.

servation or environmental groups for help). If you aren't able to find this information, think about the area you live in and what the land is like. Then think of how far you have to go before the land starts to look quite different, with the ground perhaps being more or less flat, different trees and plants showing up as you move further along, and so forth. If you haven't traveled around this place very much you may have only a vague idea of where these boundaries are, so do your best; you'll have the opportunity to find out more about this place as you continue using the exercises in this book. If you don't know the "official" name for your bioregion yet, create one that seems appropriate.

Next, look to the nearest major river; you're likely to be in its watershed. Depending on where you are, you may be very far away from that river, but eventually the rain that falls where you are flows to it. You might be closer to one of its tributaries, like a smaller river or a stream, but for now, focus on finding where the biggest river is. There may already be a name for the watershed of this river, but if not, just name it after the river itself.

After that, start looking for more local landmarks that are close to where you live. Now you can consider those smaller tributaries, along with local geological features, and even nearby flora, fauna, and fungi. Is there a particular hill that stands out in your neighborhood? Do you live in a place where one type of tree is found in unusually large numbers? Does the land you live on also support a crucial population of an endangered native animal species? You can even add in the human element to all this, though keep it in relation to the other beings here as well.

Here are a couple of examples of bioregional addresses:

Tōru lives near Nagai Park in Osaka, Japan. While it's an urban environment, he enjoys spending time in the park, particularly in the small piece of natural forest that's been preserved amid the development there. While he's visited other forested areas further out from the city, he considers this to be his home. He finds that Osaka lies within a bioregion called the Taiheiyo Evergreen Forests, which he finds even more appropriate to his situation. He's not very far from the Yamato River, either, and while its banks are quite full of human development, he knows the rain that falls in "his" little forest flows into its waters. He decides that his bioregional address is what he calls "Last Forest Standing," in the Yamato River Watershed, Taiheyo Evergreen Forests.

Valerie has lived in Sedona, Arizona, her entire life. She loves the red rock deserts and the many sunny days, and she feels like she's hiked almost every trail and dry streambed within fifty miles. Wanting to have a deeper connection with the land, she starts researching bioregionalism. Sedona is within the Arizona-New Mexico Mountains bioregion, and since she's in a desert, she wants to especially focus on watersheds. The nearest waterway is Oak

Creek, which flows into the Verde River, itself a tribu-
tary of the Salt River. From there the water flows into the
Gila River, and then into the great Colorado River which
carved the Grand Canyon. She considers all of these wa-
ters to be important in the dry southwest deserts, but
for short, she says she lives in the Oak Creek Watershed,
Arizona-New Mexico Mountains, Colorado River Water-
shed, Southwest Deserts.

You're allowed some creativity when creating your bioregional address. You might choose to only identify the very closest landmark and the largest bioregion, and nothing in between (such as "Wolf's Den Hill, Atlantic Maritime Bioregion"). You could identify your address completely by waterways (Valerie in the example above could live in "Oak-Verde-Salt-Gila-Colorado Watershed System"). Those who name their homes could even place their abode at the beginning of their address ("Kestrel's Loft, Sacramento River Watershed, Central California Valley").

Hitting the Books,
and Websites, and Museums...

Once you've identified your bioregion, it's time to get to know it in more detail. I'd like to offer you some basic "getting to know you" exercises that can help you learn more about your home territory. There are additional exercises in the bioregional chapters in *New Paths to Animal Totems* and *Plant and Fungus Totems*, so if you have those books you're welcome to draw on that material as well.

I recommend starting with some research: look for articles, books, websites, and other resources on local biology, geology, and other natural sciences. You may also wish to consult local natural history museums, university science departments, and nature organizations like your local Audubon Society. (Appendix C has some more detailed suggestions for getting started with your research.) I've offered the following questions as inspiration for your explorations. You don't have to answer all of them right away, and you can jump around the list however you like. You may even find that one particular topic really catches your attention; feel free to take the time to explore it in detail.

- What sorts of native animals live in your bioregion? Which ones are here year-round, and which ones leave for part of the year, and why? How many months out of the year are insects and other invertebrates active outdoors? Which ones have adapted best to humans living in their territory and which have fared the worst?

- What are some of the native plants in your bioregion? Which ones stay green year-round? What are their lifespans like—which ones only live a year, and which live many? Which ones are edible, and which ones are poisonous? What part of the year could you garden outdoors in?

- What fungi live in your ecoregion? Which ones produce fruiting bodies (mushrooms)? What types of fungi live in the soil, and what lives in rotting logs and other decaying matter? Which are considered edible, and which are

you complete me ♡   ♡   ♡

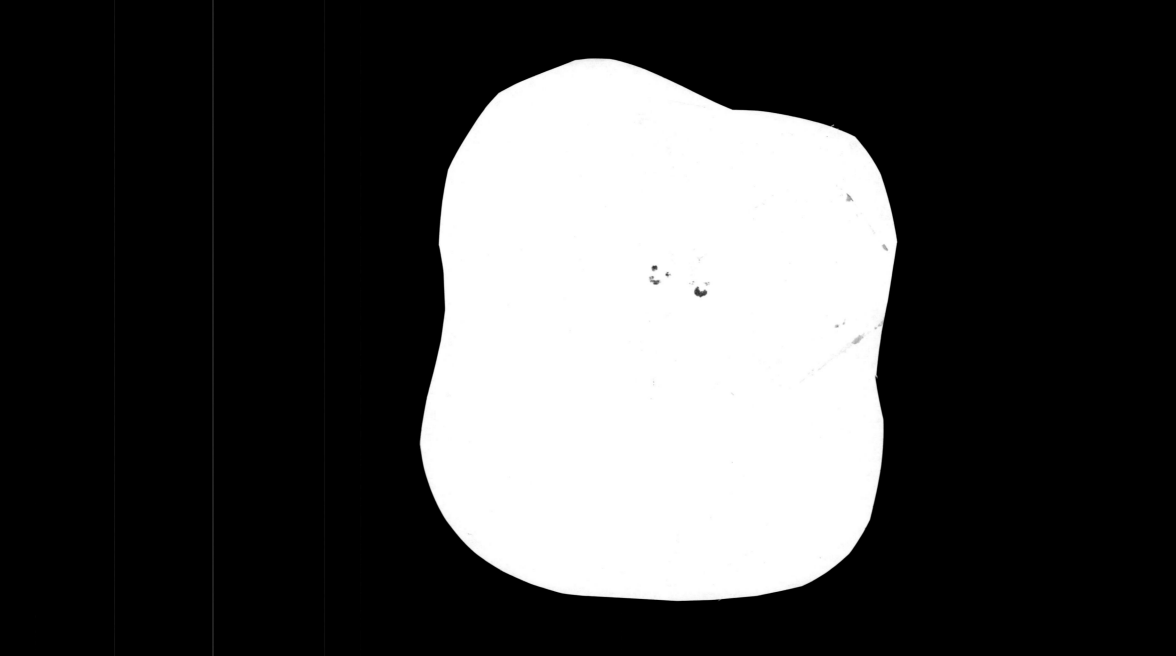

poisonous (and especially which poisonous ones look like edible ones)?

- What are some of the introduced or invasive animals, plants, and fungi in your area? How did they get there and when did they arrive? How much of an impact do they have on the bioregion, and what native species are they competing with? What is being done to remove them?

- Which species used to live in your area one hundred years ago that aren't there now? Five hundred years? Ten thousand years? A million? Fifty million? More?

- What is the geological history of your bioregion? How old are the landforms and waterways and how were they formed? What landforms and waterways did they replace? Where are the oldest and newest stones in your bioregion to be found, and when and how did they form? What are the highest and lowest elevations in your bioregion?

- How deep is the soil where you live? Is it more clay-heavy or sandy? Does it absorb water easily, or does water tend to run off of it? How many worms can you find in one cubic foot of soil?

- What watershed do you live in? What's the biggest river in your bioregion, and what smaller rivers, streams, springs, and other waters flow into it? What lakes and ponds are nearby, and are they natural or human-made? How often do these waters flood, and what's the highest watermark recorded? Have any human alterations been made to these waterways?

- If you live near an ocean or sea, how much does the water level change from low tide to high tide? Do the tides affect any of the living beings in or around the water?

- What are the farthest points north and south on the eastern horizon the sun and moon rise throughout the year? What about setting on the western horizon? If the sun or moon isn't visible due to cloud cover, what features (natural or human-made) could you use to tell the four cardinal directions? What would you use if you were ten miles in another direction? Twenty miles? More?

- On a clear night, what constellations are you able to see? Which would you see six months from now? (If you live in a city, head out to a more rural area if you're able. The difference in what stars you're able to see can be very dramatic.)

- When do you start noticing one season changing to the next, and how closely are those changes related to the solstices and equinoxes? What's the coldest it usually gets throughout the year? The hottest? What's the average yearly rainfall as well as the average for each month? How many sunny days do you get in an average year? What direction does the wind usually come from, and what's the highest wind speed ever recorded in your bioregion? Are there geological features or waterways that change weather patterns coming in?

- What are the natural phenomena considered to be the most dangerous to humans? (Examples: earthquakes, tornados, drought, floods, etc.) What are the natural processes that cause these phenomena, and how can humans better prepare for and coexist with them?

- Who are the people indigenous to your bioregion, and do they still live there? What was and is their relationship to that place? Who else lives there, and how have they related to the land and its earlier inhabitants?

- How have humans changed the land? How have they changed where the rain flows when it falls? What animals, plants, and fungi thrive there? Which don't? Have any changed the shape of the land itself? How aware are all the people living in your bioregion today of their impact on it and its nonhuman residents? Is there much effort to improve the land and address any environmental problems it may face?

- If you have lived in the same place for a number of years, how has it changed since you first moved there? What has remained the same? What is under threat of damage or destruction? What may be restored and replenished?

Be aware that the answers to these questions will vary from place to place; even a location a quarter mile from your home may be different in some ways. You may wish to take a survey of several locations within your bioregion and compare and contrast the results you get. If you want to test your knowledge once you've done some research, I recommend the Ehoah Bioregional Quiz written by Rua Lupa, found at ehoah.weebly .com/bioregional-quiz.html.

Finally, don't believe you have to be an expert on your bioregion. There's no final test here, and you're welcome to explore your world at your own pace. Understanding your bioregion is a way to deepen your connection to both nonhuman nature and the spiritual beings that populate it for the benefit of all involved.

———

Sadie always thought she knew a lot about her bioregion. After all, she can name several of the birds that routinely show up in her yard, she recognizes that the soil in her garden has a lot of clay and rocks in it, and she can name a couple of nearby rivers and mountains, which is more than a lot of her friends can do! But as she begins to study her bioregion in more depth, she realizes there are a lot of things she didn't know. She learns that the closest mountains were caused by tectonic uplift, and that her area routinely experiences very small earthquakes still, too small to be noticed by anyone but seismological instruments. And while she knows some birds and other animals as well as domestic plants, she can only name a few wild plants besides trees, and precisely three mushrooms, two of which come from the grocery store, not her bioregion. Rather than being discouraged, she feels motivated to find out more about this place she lives in.

Boots (Shoes) (Wheels) (Etc.) on the Ground

Now that you have more information about your bioregion, it's time to start applying it. I routinely recommend getting out and wandering around the neighborhood (if possible) or other location to people who want to know more about their bioregion. It's one thing to know about a place in theory, but looking at pictures on the computer isn't the same as observing sights, smells, and sounds from a window, or getting outside when possible, too.

Chances are that as you've made progress with your research, the things you've learned have started to slip into your perception of your environment. You might find yourself noticing plants you've learned about as you walk past them, remembering which ones are native and which ones aren't. Or you may pay more attention to insects than you had before; you might not be able to name them exactly but you still find yourself at least trying to place what taxonomic order they're in.

You can also make a more concerted effort to apply your knowledge. Whenever you're outside or even just looking out the window for a few minutes, start deliberately recalling everything you know about the living beings, landforms, and other natural features you're observing. See if the animals' behavior matches what you've learned or if you notice something new. Take note of any plants you recognize—and any you don't and would like to identify later. If you go up or down a hill, see if you can identify how that hill was made. Even if you're just out for a couple of minutes, walking from your car or bus to your destination, or running a local errand around the corner from home, you may be amazed by how educational an experience it can be.

———

Bo has always enjoyed hiking in the large park on the outskirts of his city; it's his favorite way to relax and a lot more fun than going to the gym. This is his first time back since he started studying the geology of his bioregion, and almost immediately he starts noticing details about the trail he's on that he hadn't paid much attention to before. He recognizes the stone cliffs along part of the trail are limestone, and after taking a little time to study them more closely he finds a few small fossil shells. He also recognizes that a part of the hillside further along the trail has been displaced by uplift; layers of rock that should be horizontal instead angle upward. While it does take him longer to complete his hike, by the time he's done he feels like he understands the concepts he's been studying better now that he's seen them illustrated in real life.

Your Bioregional Map

This next exercise asks you to get a little more creative. You're going to be creating a map of your bioregion, and you have a few potential options for your medium:

- Create a map from scratch. It can be to scale if you like, though you can also accentuate certain areas or otherwise make it more abstract. Feel free to use whatever artistic medium you like, though make sure it's one you can add to later as needed.

- Get a big paper map of your city/town/other local area. Modify it using markers, sticky notes, or whatever other method you like. You can also make a reusable version by laminating the paper map and then using dry erase markers on it.

- Use Google Map's customization options to make a virtual map of your bioregion complete with virtual markers and other pertinent information.

You can customize your map any number of ways. You might start by outlining your bioregion (there are maps online that can show you the boundaries of your bioregion/ecoregion) and then marking down important information from your research on the map such as important landforms and how they were made or the historical and modern ranges of a particular animal species. After every walk or excursion, you can use the map to record what you observed and when you observed it. You can even use the map to plan future trips out into your bioregion, places you really want to check out, seasonal wildlife-related events, and more.

A customized map is a great way to keep track of your progress as you get to know your bioregion better. If you color code different elements of the bioregion, such as brown for animals, green for plants, blue for water, and so on, you can then use your collected data to determine if there are certain things you're studying more than others. If you find that you've accumulated a lot of information on geology but not much on fungi, you may wish to spend a little more time on the latter—or it may point toward a desire to specialize in the former!

We'll work more with the bioregional map later, but for now just focus on setting it up.

Being at Home in Your Bioregion

I mentioned in the last chapter my dissatisfaction with the idea that humans are no longer a part of nature and how it furthers a sense of alienation from the rest of the world. One way to counteract that is by consciously identifying yourself and your home as part of your bioregion, even if you live in the middle of a densely populated city.

If you've already researched the answers to some of the questions earlier in this chapter, you may have a good idea of how buildings, roads, and other human creations have changed your bioregion. For the purposes of this ritual, you'll need to be especially familiar with the effects your apartment, house, or dwelling has on the land (and water, if applicable) around it. In addition to direct observation of your immediate neighborhood, you may also wish to imagine what the place looked like before humans dramatically changed it (in its "natural" state, if you will) to help you get a better idea of how much *has* changed.

Once you have a pretty good understanding of the above, the next step is to state your intention to be a good neighbor in your bioregion. You can symbolically do this through the following ritual, which you're welcome to change as you see fit.

Set up a place where you won't be disturbed for at least an hour. You can make this place at home, a special place in your bioregion, or maybe one you feel especially drawn to or where you've made good memories. If you work from home, try to be by a window if possible. You can even do this in a place where there will be other people if they're just strangers going about their own business like at a park or hiking trail; if you're worried about looking weird in front of others, read the spoken parts silently in your head and do your best to be less obvious about the ritual's active portions.

If possible, bring or find a small item that reminds you of your place in the bioregion.[3] It might be a stone, pine cone, dried leaf, a vial of local water (your tap water is a good reminder that you rely on the bioregion!), or a jar of soil. Or you could bring your bioregional map with you, or another representation of part or all of the bioregion. It could even be a book that helped you in your research or assisted in strengthening your connection to this place, or a photo you took of something special in the bioregion.

You will also want to bring some little piece of yourself you can give as an offering to the land. A bit of your hair is a good choice, though if that's not possible save a few fingernail

---

3. Keep in mind that some places such as city, state, or national parks may not allow visitors to take natural items out of the park so as to keep people from damaging the place. Please respect these boundaries and leave the flowers and pebbles where they are. Later in the book I'll discuss how to create a link to the land without taking anything native to it.

clippings.[4] This creates an exchange with the land in which you leave a bit of yourself there as thanks for the piece of it you take with you.

Once you're ready to begin, make yourself comfortable either standing or sitting. Spend a few moments focusing on your breathing and letting the tension drain out of your body. Clear your mind; if thoughts arise, let them drift by like leaves on a stream or clouds in the sky. Next, hold up the item representing the bioregion and meditate for a few moments on where it came from, why you brought that particular thing with you, and all the things you've learned about your bioregion. Then, hold it against the ground in front of you and say (or think to yourself):

I am human, Homo sapiens, *far-ranging and curious.*

I am human, Homo sapiens, *destructive and dangerous.*

I am of those who have forgotten our place in the world,

We who wander, rootless, never at rest,

---

4. I recognize that for some people leaving your hair or nail clippings around may seem like a bad idea, as there are certain beliefs that state that others can use these parts of you to curse you or otherwise send malignant energy your way. However, the land doesn't give up its offerings easily, and this ritual is designed to transfer whatever essence of "you" is attached to these things to the land itself as part of the process, which leaves the physical remnants "empty." Sure, someone could still ostensibly steal your hair or nails and leave them at the scene of a murder, but it's exceptionally improbable, to the point where you're more likely to be attacked by a herd of stampeding lemmings than be framed for a crime you didn't commit. As to leaving your hair and nails around being purportedly gross, it's a teensy, perfectly biodegradable part of you that won't last more than a few weeks in the wild at most, and you probably shed more hair than that just walking around on a regular basis. I'll talk more about offerings later, too.

Only a few of us remember what "home" means.

I want to come back home.

I want to bring us back home.

I want to remember what home is.

I ask that you, [name of bioregion], *help me find my way.*

I want to make my shelter a home within you.

I want my walls to be rooted within you.

I want the path from my door to always lead to you.

Let this [stone, map, etc.] *remind me of what I must do to help create that bond.*

Let it remind me of the work I have to do, and the listening I must offer you.

Let it be a center of my home that I create within you,

And a reminder that I never truly left; I only thought I did.

Next, take the hair or nails and scatter them across the ground (or if you prefer, find a place nearby to hide them safely away, such as under a rock or in a hole in a tree). As you do, say or think the following:

As you have given to me, so I give back to you. I give to you a piece of myself made from the food you fed me, the proteins I pulled from your soil through the local food I ate. I have transformed it, left my imprint on it, and now I offer you that piece of myself as a promise. I promise to be mindful of my place here within you. I promise to do my best to be a good neighbor to the other living beings

here and to the land and the waters and the sky. In doing
so, may I learn to be as generous as you.

Pick up the item representing the bioregion and hold it in
your hand (or otherwise keep it in close contact with you) all
the way home. Then let the first thing you do when you walk
in the door be placing it in a special spot you've prepared for
it. It can be one particular shelf, a quiet corner of a room, or
hanging over your bed—whatever works best for you. Try to
make it somewhere where you'll see it every day. If you remember, pick it up or look at it at least once a day as a reminder; you might even make it a part of your routine first
thing in the morning or when you get ready to go to bed at
night. You can also incorporate it into some of the exercises
and rituals appearing later in this book; let the object be a tiny
symbolic microcosm of your bioregion that carries the land's
energy wherever it is. I'll discuss how to work with this energy
and connection more later.[5]

You may wish to meditate with your object now and then
at home. While holding it, try visualizing the energy it carries
expanding beyond the item itself, and then filling your entire
home, and then expanding outward to meet the energy outside, linking the indoors to the outdoors. Feel how your home
is your nest or den, a little place giving you shelter within the

---

5. Please note that when I say "energy" I don't mean something like electricity, but a more esoteric sort of energy. You can consider it a nonphysical
or even magical force if you like, though it's also perfectly acceptable to
look at it in a more symbolic manner as the representation of the qualities
or "feel" of a place. Sensing that energy serves as a good reminder of your
memories of the location, which have a power of their own.

greater bioregion. It is a dwelling created by human hands, but it is as dependent on the bioregion as any burrow or spider's web. Imagine the walls don't separate you from your bioregion any more than the twigs in a nest or soil in a den. Then place the item back in its place and let it continue to anchor that energetic connection in your home.

———

Now that you've gotten to know your bioregion, let's find out more about the totems of the fungi, flora, and fauna (among others) who live there alongside you.

Three

Introducing the Totems Themselves

Our world is populated by a wide variety of living beings and other phenomena. We're most familiar with the physical animals, plants, and the forests, fields, and other ecosystems in which they live and thrive. Each part of nature has its own individual spirits, whether they're embodied in live animals and other biological beings or within physical stones and waters. There are also "disembodied" nature spirits, those that either no longer have physical form or never had one at all but are still an integral part of the natural world. Cultures around the world and throughout the history of our species have acknowledged, honored, feared, and placated these spiritual beings and their physical counterparts.

I'm not here to talk about individual spirits, however. Some of them can certainly be powerful allies if we make good relations with them, but they're not the totems I had in mind. A totem represents all of the members of a given species or phenomenon, physical and otherwise. The totem Barn Owl, for example, was never itself born into a physical body. But Barn Owl watches over all barn owls of the past, present, and future, as well as all the barn owl spirits that have never had bodies themselves.

Before we move on, I'd like to introduce some of the types of totems you may be working with as you use this book. Traditionally, totemism and similar systems in indigenous cultures have largely dealt with animals, plants, fungi, and stones (depending on the individual culture, of course). The role of these totems has varied from a set of symbols akin to surnames that organize the people into groups and govern who may marry whom, to individual allies and protective spirits, to beings that watch over secret societies and other sacred groups within a community. When I write about totemism, here and otherwise, I am not speaking from any indigenous perspective—quite the contrary, I am a white girl from the Midwest, raised as a Roman Catholic and self-and-spirit-taught as a Neopagan since 1996. I use the term "totem" not in its original Ojibwe context, but in the broader definition the word has come to take in the English language. What I describe here is my own creation based on years of practice, experimentation, and direct work with the totems themselves, as well as notes I've traded with other neototemist practitioners.

I will share anecdotes throughout this book, but my experiences should not be seen as holy writ or some indication of a totem's meaning. I don't put totem dictionaries in my books specifically because I want people to forge their own relationships with the totems rather than saying, "Well Lupa said that Domestic Horse taught her about independence? That means Horse means independence universally!" What a totem tells you may not be what it tells me, and I'd rather you not miss out on the sometimes amazing and terrifying but *always* rewarding experience of discovering totems for yourself.

I've already written extensively on animal, plant, and fungus totems in previous works (there's a list of those at the beginning of this book). Now I'd like to at least introduce some of the types of totems you may be working with in your bioregional work.

Biological Totems

The totems we're most familiar with are those of biological beings. The three main groups of biological totems are animal, plant, and fungus totems. These totems each watch over an individual species. It's important to make these distinctions. Spectacled Bear is a different totem than Polar Bear, for example, and while they may have certain ursine qualities in common their experiences are vastly different overall. Therefore it is short-sighted to talk about a "Bear" totem, especially when what most people really mean is Brown Bear.

Another thing to keep in mind are odd exceptions. While various North American canid species have always interbred, in recent years coyote-wolf hybrids, or coywolves, have begun to establish themselves as a group in the Northeastern United States and other places where gray wolves have been pushed back. The few remaining wolves mated with coyotes, and these offspring then interbred with other wolves, coyotes, and each other. Coywolf is a very new totem who has been birthed as coywolves created their own unique niche; sometimes Coywolf will show up as Gray Wolf and/or Coyote, or sometimes all three will appear.

Animal Totems

These are the best known and most commonly worked with totems; they're often the easiest for us to relate to as we ourselves are animals. For millennia we've looked to them for lessons on how to behave, and we've told stories about them to teach ourselves and each other cultural morals and pass down information from generation to generation. We see a bit of ourselves in them, and hope to embody some of their qualities, too.

As some cultures have become more industrialized and distant from nature, animal totemism has often been reduced to a series of mascots or symbols on billboards and clothing. But over the past couple of decades, as interest in nature spirituality in general has increased, people have started re-exploring totemism as more than mere symbols. This is especially true for nonindigenous people (like me) who weren't raised in cultures with totemic systems, allowing us to create our own relationships with the animals based on our experiences and values.

The big, impressive animals like hawks and lions aren't the only ones who have totems. Every animal species, from *Paramecium caudatum* to the blue whale, has a totem watching over it. There are also totems for extinct species and domesticated ones. Some even include mythological animals under the totemic umbrella.[6]

Because we ourselves are animals, we often find it easiest to reach out to the totems of other animal species. They're familiar, and it's not too much of a stretch for us to imagine what another animal's experiences might be like. Many of us have a favorite animal when we're children—and a lot of us hold onto those into adulthood, too! For some, it turns out that favorite animal was in fact a totem making an early appearance in our lives. So what differentiates a favorite animal and a totem?

When I was very young, Gray Wolf came to me while I was observing the family dog, a large black German shepherd. From then on I was absolutely obsessed with wolves. I had shirts, statues, stuffed toys, and books all about gray wolves. I pretended to be a wolf whenever I played with other kids at school, even if it made no sense in the game we were playing. As I got older, I found that this "wolf-ness" was rubbing off on me. I found myself emulating wolves—usually in very clumsy imitations. I discovered Paganism and other forms of nature spirituality in my teens and began to explore totemism, at which point Gray Wolf made a more formal introduction. The totem told me how it had been with me the whole time,

---

6. While I will largely be talking about the totems of extant species and those native to this world, if you happen to meet, say, Hyaenadon Gigas or Domestic Pig as totems of your bioregion, you can still use the material in this book. They might have a little different perspective than their living and/or wild counterparts, but they may be able to give you some unique perspectives on the land.

guiding me in my floppy-eared puppy stages. Wolves were still my favorite animals, and after this meeting there was more purpose to the interest.

While we're on the subject, a question that comes up every now and then is whether *Homo sapiens* has a totem. In my experience (and you're welcome to take this with as much salt as you like), we myth-making animals were not content with just one totem to describe our complex experiences and ourselves. We acknowledge many deities with humanlike characteristics who still maintain the profound power and awe associated with the human and other natural phenomena they embody. Opinions vary as to whether each of these deities is their own independent being or whether they all reflect facets of one great divinity; needless to say, I tend to think of totems as the gods of other beings, and perhaps they see them in more nuanced, complex forms than we do.

However, there may also be much to be learned by going to the Ur-totem of our species, *Homo sapiens sapiens*. Before gods, temples, agriculture, and alphabets was the human ape. Really, there were several human apes—us, the Neanderthals and the Denisovans, and numerous other now-extinct hominins. We were the only survivors to this day, and our totem still waits at the root of our DNA for us to remember ourselves and who we were before we fell into our current spiral of self-centered delusion and outward destruction. I haven't done much work with this totem yet, so this is all I'll say about it for now.

Plant Totems

Most writings on plants in spiritual practices are focused on using parts of the physical plants for our benefit either through herbalism or mind-altering entheogens. Some may acknowledge the spirits of the individual plants, but rarely are their totems addressed, a practice due to human bias toward animals as exemplary living beings, where plants as only part of the scenery. In fact, the term "plant blindness" was created to describe this phenomenon; plants are simply not *seen* let alone appreciated for their crucial places in ecosystems and their unique evolutionary history. When we walk through the forest or fields, we gasp with joy when we see a single bird fly up out of the grass, but we don't take time to explore the grass itself or any of its other plant neighbors.

I started working with plant totems after my move to Portland; the animal totems that greeted me encouraged me almost immediately to start talking to their plant and other nonanimal neighbors. Some, like Douglas Fir, were new to me; others, like Red and White Clovers, had been around most of my life without me realizing it. They were instrumental in helping me appreciate totemism on a bioregional level.

Working with plant totems is different from animal totem work in some ways, and a lot of this has to do with how plants view the world. For the most part, they're stationary beings once their seeds settle into a patch of soil. However, there's still plenty of movement up and out as they try to get as much sunlight as they can. In my experience, this tends to give them a viewpoint of depth rather than breadth of knowledge; plants put down roots and get to know one place for life. No surprise, then, that they were some of the strongest supporters of my getting to know my Oregon home in as much detail as possible!

Where animal totems often seek us out actively, plant totems are more likely to wait patiently for us to pay attention. I find that the state of soft fascination referred to earlier works especially well for catching these more subtle signals. When I allow my perception to relax, rather than being bombarded by stimuli, I'm more able to notice when a plant totem may be trying to get my attention. For instance, when I first began hiking in the Columbia River Gorge, I was often overwhelmed by sightings of ravens and mule deer and the Douglas fir and Western red cedar trees towering overhead. It took a while for me to settle my perception down enough that I started to notice the less obvious parts of the ecosystem I was walking through, like banana slugs and tiny white shelf fungi. It was in this stillness I was able to hear the soft voice of Western Maidenhair Fern hidden in the undergrowth, one of the first plant totems to teach me the value of quiet communication.

We're a little lower on the list of a plant totem's priorities. While we require plants to live as omnivore, they could do quite well without us humans, so long as there were other animals to produce carbon dioxide for them to breathe and decaying flesh for fertilizer. The fact that some plants can feed us is less out of altruism and more about the plants using us. Tasty fruit surrounds seeds that animals then spread around in droppings; the fruit wasn't produced exclusively for our benefit. It's also the case that while some plant totems—especially the totems of domesticated plants—enjoy working with us, others seem ambivalent at best. Often it will be up to us to start a conversation with them and give them reasons to work with us.

Because plants figured out different solutions to the problems life throws at all beings, a plant totem's perspective and manner of communicating with us may seem quite alien at times. Working with plant totems is often an exercise in stretching the mind, and it may involve everything from communicating through scent (chemical signals are big communicators for plants) to trying to be patient with long-lived tree totems that wonder why we can't just outlive our problems.

There are other ways in which plant totems differ from their animal counterparts, but for the most part it all boils down to a completely different set of evolutionary tactics for surviving and thriving in a multitude of environments. With patience and a little humility, we can reach out to them and create just as strong a set of relationships as with our animal totems.

Fungus Totems

If plants are often ignored in totemism and elsewhere, fungi are all but completely forgotten. With the exception of some writings on hallucinogenic fungi like psilocybin mushrooms, fungi are usually lumped together with plants under the too-broad heading "mushrooms" or aren't mentioned at all. What's more, fungi are often demonized; outside of mushrooms, we're more likely to hear about the medical problems caused by athlete's foot (*Tricophyton* sp.), ringworm (*Tinea* sp.), yeast infections (*Candida* sp.), or the health problems caused by buildings infested with black mold (*Stachybotrys* sp.).

In reality, fungi are absolutely necessary to our existence. Several species normally live in or on our bodies, and we cannot survive without them. Almost all plants, including ones we eat or feed to our livestock, have symbiotic relationships with fungi that are intertwined with their roots and help them absorb nutrients and survive in harsh conditions. Fungi break down rotting plants and animals and return those nutrients to the food cycle; commercial agriculture involves chemicals that kill off the resident fungi, necessitating the use of harsh chemical fertilizers to make sure the crops grow big and fast enough in the fungi's absence.

The lessons fungus totems have to show us differ from those of plants in many ways. While fungi appear to be rooted in place much like plants, the mushrooms we see popping up overnight are simply the temporary reproductive parts. The main part of the organism exists as an extensive network of filaments throughout the soil, decaying log, or other substrate the fungus grows in.

One of the most important things I learned in dealing with anyone—human, fungus, or otherwise—came from the totem Fly Agaric. The bright red cap of its mushroom is the well-known "toadstool" in picture books and Nintendo games worldwide. Siberian shamans and more recently psychonauts also consume it as a hallucinogen in spite of its toxicity. Fly Agaric isn't especially happy about its perception as a way to get high (even for spiritual purposes) and especially resents newer attitudes that commodify it rather than treating it as a valuable part of its ecosystem only to be taken out with great reverence. It was Fly Agaric that really brought home to me the fact that most of its life cycle is spent in the soil, helping plants to grow and offering nourishment to tiny microscopic beings that further break down decaying matter. In our very first conversation, this totem emphasized that the decay cycle was its most important job and that we humans would do well to remember that. My takeaway was a crucial lesson in not making nature spirituality so human-centered; Fly Agaric and other fungus totems have a lot more to do than feeding hungry animals and their spiritual proclivities.

Unlike plants, fungi don't need sunlight to survive. You may be surprised to know that fungi are actually more closely related to us animals than they are to plants—we share a common ancestor that existed long after plants had split off from our part of the evolutionary tree. In my experience, these two facts further contribute to the fungus totems' more grounded approach. Plants may be rooted, but their totems have a bit of an obsession with growing higher and upward, competing for sunlight. Fungus totems are less fussy about solutions to problems; after all, fungi will grow in everything from digestive tracts to dung to rotting carcasses. If you want a practical and down to earth perspective, talk to a fungus totem.

And due to the fact that a lot of fungi aren't good for us health-wise, either ingested or inhaled, they're reminders that being a part of nature means taking the bad with the good. They're pretty unapologetic about that harsh lesson, too. I once asked Destroying Angel, the totem of a notoriously poisonous fungus, why its mushroom was so deadly. "Well," it said, "it keeps you from eating them before they've spawned, doesn't it?"

One thing that fungus totems do have in common with their plant counterparts is that they're often quieter than animal totems. In my experience, if an animal totem wants to get my attention in a meditation or otherwise, it'll come and find me. Fungus and plant totems, on the other hand, tend to wait to be noticed; much like their physical children, they often go overlooked. When they do try to open communication, the ways they talk tend to be not so much vocal and verbal as through intuition; when I work with plant and fungus totems I tend to "feel" rather than "hear" them, and I'll talk more about that later in this chapter. So we (as human animals ourselves) need to be more proactive in making contact with them, as well as learning the unique ways in which they communicate with us. On the other hand, keep in mind that many fungi have a tendency toward grumpiness, so it may take a while for them to warm up to you.

A Quick Note About Lichens

Lichens are a special case. Lichens are composite organisms made of a fungus and an algae (though some lichens have a cyanobacteria, or plant-like bacteria, instead of the algae). They're classified biologically with fungi since the fungus in a lichen provides the being's structure and main body, while the algae is sort of a photosynthetic add-on. It's a very important add-on, though; if a lichen is separated into its fungus and algae components, the fungus loses its shape. So the algae gives form to the raw material of the fungus's body.

Lichen totems have a similarly dual nature. When I work with lichen totems, sometimes the totem of the lichen itself will show up. Other times, I work with the totems of the individual species of fungus and algae that make up the physical lichen. At times all three will appear at various points in my meditation or ritual. It seems to be primarily a preference on the part of the individual lichen totem whether or not the fungus and plant totems are involved.

The various appearances of lichen totems may also be related to a point the totem wishes to make. The totem Oak Moss Lichen once appeared to me initially as itself but then split into its corresponding fungus and algae totems. It did this because it wanted to emphasize that we too are complex beings with many parts and layers and elements that all come together to create us as individuals.

There are plenty of biological beings besides animals, plants, and fungi, such as bacteria, protozoa, and archaea. These are generally too tiny for us to see, and outside of microbiology few of us know much about them. You're welcome to work with them if you like, but I won't be addressing them much in this book for sake of space and time. Many of the concepts in this book can be used to connect with microscopic totems, so feel free to experiment if you like!

Land Totems

In addition to the biological totems I've already discussed, there is an additional, broader group of totems: the land totems. Some people may debate the use of the term "totem" to refer to these beings, either because they aren't associated with biological beings like animals, or because some cultures have referred to the embodiments of natural phenomena as "spirits" instead. In my personal experience the overarching guardians and caretakers of different types of land and water formations, natural forces, and places have the same general characteristics as animal, plant, and fungus totems. For the purposes of my practice and writing here, I use the term "totem" as an umbrella covering all of these. It's a bit of a semantics debate to be sure, and if at the end of the book you decide you wish to use different terms for any of the beings I discuss here while still using the concepts I describe, you're more than welcome to do so.

These are the totems of what we'd consider the nonliving parts of nature. They're the totems of minerals and waterways, of land-shaping forces and weather patterns, of soil and sand. Animal, plant, and fungus totems are defined through individual species that evolved over time; while individual members of those species may live in very different places—gray wolves in Mexico versus in Russia, for example—every one of them shares a single common ancestor and has essentially the same DNA makeup minus a few regional and individual quirks. Land totems, on the other hand, are more defined by certain patterns of natural formation and other nonbiological phenomena that have the same results each time. Sandstone always forms when sand and other tiny mineral particles (usually quartz or feldspar) are bound together with a natural mineral cement. Quartzite always forms from sandstone made from quartz that is then subjected to great heat and pressure through tectonic activity.

Remember in the introduction when I said that totems are made of several different components in addition to natural history, including relationships their physical counterparts have with the rest of their ecosystem? It's the same way with land totems. Take the metal gold. Its totem watches over every atom of gold in existence. But the totem Gold also includes the complex relationships that humanity has had with gold over the millennia, good and bad, from its value and beauty, to the warnings that gold can lead to temptation, to the harmful mining practices often used to extract it from the ground. It also is made of the various forms that gold has been sculpted into over time, from devotional statues to electronic circuits, and the meanings behind these creations. So, like animal and other biological totems, land totems are more than just the physical rock, wind, or water they watch over.

Whereas an animal species has one totem associated with it, other parts of nature may have several. There are totems of specific types of mineral and different sorts of rock, but there are also totems of the erosive and volcanic and other forces that shaped these stones. When you hold a piece of obsidian in your hand, you're holding a connection to multiple totems—Silica is the totem of the mineral it's made of, Volcano is the totem of the geologic phenomenon that created it, and Obsidian is its "self" totem.

If this is too confusing, you're welcome to work with the most immediate totem, that of the stone or other mineral you're working with. Just keep in mind that they're more complex than gemstone dictionaries make them out to be, and other factors—like the quartz that the stone tiger's eye is made from, or the heat and pressure that caused the metamorphosis—may come into play. Again, you have to create your own relationships with the totem—what Tiger's Eye told the writer of such-and-such book may not be what it wants to tell you.

You might think that the sun and moon are totems as well, in and of themselves. However, they are individual celestial bodies that happen to have a direct effect on the planet. Most stars and moons are too far away to even be visible, let alone interact with us and our world. But we can consider the totems Star and Moon as those that watch over the sun-star that provides the sunlight that bathes our world, and the satellite-moon whose gravity draws the tides to and fro. Even though most of their physical counterparts are much further out in the galaxy, we can still consider Star and Moon to be land totems because of the contributions two of their children make to our planet. And, of course, our own Earth is watched over by the totem Planet.[7]

Going smaller rather than bigger, it is possible to break totemism down even more finely; there are totems of the individual elements like carbon and oxygen, as well as of molecules,

---

7. It could be argued that "Planet" and "Moon" could just be lumped in with "Asteroid" and so forth under the totem "Space Rock," especially in the wake of the controversy over whether Pluto is a planet or not. I believe totemism is in large part human conversation with the rest of nature, and so we do contribute our categorization to the matters at hand.

and parts of atoms. Even subatomic particles have their own mysterious totems we're only just getting to know. The perspectives of these very small, large, or strange totems may seem quite alien indeed (pun only partly intended). Planet, for example, is used to working with entire worlds, ranging from tiny little balls of ice in outer reaches of solar systems to gaseous globes too toxic for us to ever approach. While it's aware that on one little blue planet, Earth, the well-developed life-system is shifting drastically right now, it takes a more whole-world view rather than being concerned with the goings-on of individual life forms. My attempts to work with these great celestial totems hasn't gotten me particularly far, much like one cell in my body trying to get my attention may be unsuccessful. I've had similar troubles working with the very smallest, like Proton and Charm Quark and the totems of other atomic particles.

A totem practice can be quite complicated, as you can see. For the sake of this book, I'll primarily be sticking with land totems whose physical counterparts can generally be seen with the average naked eye and are largely confined to our planet (and with which I've actually been able to communicate). If you happen to connect with something not included here, you can still try using the material in this book to work with it.

Natural forces also have their totems. Gravity has a totem that embodies not only the gravitational pull of the earth, moon, and sun, but also all the research and storytelling we've made about gravity, even the semi-apocryphal tale of Isaac Newton "discovering" gravity after an apple fell on his head. (It actually didn't hit him, for what it's worth; he just observed it fall to the ground and that got him thinking about why.)

Erosion is another totem that comes into play quite a bit. When I spend time in the Columbia River Gorge, I may come into contact with a whole host of totems, not all of which are biological. Take the Columbia River itself. River is, of course, one of the prevailing totems. So is Basalt, Volcano, and Flood brought forth by Glacier. And there's Erosion, still wearing down the stone to this day through the river and the rain and the stomp of hiking boots on the soil.

Land totems can be very difficult to contact at times, especially those that don't make use of us for their own ends. Erosion likes to reform the land into new shapes and will make use of any handy tool. When an elk goes leaping down a hillside or a large tree is uprooted by the wind, Erosion is there to break down the edges of the soil and create new configurations. Volcano, on the other hand, couldn't care less about us no matter how many offerings we toss into the lava. We may plead with deities that put a bit more anthropomorphism into the volcanoes themselves, but the *totem* Volcano is only interested in relieving pressure by whatever means necessary.

―――

Regina is a geologist whose love of the land started with a childhood love of rock hounding. From clear quartz crystals to shiny pieces of pyrite, the wide variety of minerals captured her imagination from a young age and never re-

ally left her. She's expanded her collection quite a bit over the years, but she still prizes her very first rock, a small piece of fossilized wood. For her fortieth birthday, Regina goes on a weekend meditation retreat to learn more self-care skills; one of the meditations asks participants to bring something with strong sentimental value, so she brings the petrified wood with her. During that meditation, she imagines a giant prehistoric conifer tree falling into a swamp and then settling into the mud at the bottom. The tree glows slightly as it transforms from wood to stone, tiny bits of mineral replacing the atoms of lignin, cellulose, and other biological substances. The glow then coalesces into the form of a woman of indeterminate age. She smiles and holds out her hand. Regina's little petrified wood is there, and as she takes it from the glowing woman it continues to glow. When Regina comes out of her meditation, she feels as though she has been shown some secret that exists beyond the physical process of fossilization itself, and she wonders what else the woman in her meditation might be able to teach her.

Totemic Potpourri

In the next chapter I'll talk about how to find your bioregional totems. Before that, however, I'd like to cover a few more of the basics of totemism. A number of questions frequently arise when teaching people about nonindigenous totemism. As always, the answers that follow are based on my own experience, so take them with as much salt as you like.

Are totems "real" or are they just a figment of my imagination?

As far as I'm concerned, it doesn't especially matter. I've spent almost two decades working with totems, and I gave up long ago trying to prove they exist as independent beings outside of my own experience or some collective consciousness. I speak with them as though they are their own beings, but if it turned out that it was all an elaborate play of my imagination, I wouldn't be especially bothered.

What's more important to me is how totemism affects my life and the world around me. If my practice and my relationships with the totems are making me a better person and making me a more effective steward of the environment, I'm doing things right. Whether that's due to spiritual beings or an ongoing story I tell in my mind seems irrelevant to me. (Of course, this does not prevent you from having a different opinion on the matter.)

Does every animal/plant/fungus have a totem, or only certain ones?

In my experience, every species of living being has a totem, as do the various minerals, chemicals, forces, and other phenomena of nature. This includes extinct beings, microscopic ones, and there are even totems of interstellar nature. Keep in mind that the extinct totems no longer have a physical link to our world, and so their perspective on what we experience may seem *very* alien to us, especially if the extinction was a long time ago. I did some work with dinosaur totems, and while we can agree on certain things like "mass extinction events are no fun," the ones I talked to were often positively baffled by peculiarly human behaviors (to include our mad rush toward the sixth mass extinction event). On the other hand, age does have some benefits of perspective, and the late Cretaceous totems who saw their species destroyed in the K-T event (when a giant asteroid hit the Earth and wiped out much of the life on it) had a lot to say about how much we were taking the planet for granted.

Some people have asked me whether fantastic beings have totems as well, such as Jackalope or Unicorn. In my opinion, it's mostly a matter of semantics. The archetypal beings who watch over mythological animals and the like have much the same role as their "normal" counterparts—watching over their young, embodying the stories we tell about them, and so forth. It's up to you whether you want to consider these as totems or assign a different name to them.

Does everyone have a totem?

While it's possible for anyone to try working with totems, not everyone automatically has one assigned to them. There's not some Bureau of Totemic Guidance that determines which totem will adopt each newborn baby. Many people do not follow spiritual paths that include totems; some people in Pagan or nature-based paths find they work better with other sorts of beings like individual spirits, fey, and so forth. If you work through this book and absolutely cannot make a connection with any totem, it could be that other beings are better suited for you or that your totem(s) don't feel quite ready to make themselves known to you just yet. Don't worry—I've known people who didn't find their first totem until they were well into their sixties. There's no such thing as "too late," only "just right."

I also want to reiterate that what I refer to as "totemism" here is not the same as indigenous totemisms worldwide, whether in the Americas, Europe, Australia, and elsewhere. Indigenous totemisms tend to be group-based, so in those cultures it can be generally said that yes, everyone has a totem associated with their family, just as in many places everyone has a last name they're given at birth. They may have additional guardian or guiding spirits throughout their lives.

Nonindigenous totemism like what I write about blends these two concepts out of necessity. As a white American who grew up in the Midwest in a Catholic family that had little to do with nature, let alone nature spirituality, I had no conception of a family totem. It could be that Gray Wolf, who came to me at such a young age, is a long-lost familial totem, but without a lot of research I can't verify that for sure. However, I allied myself with these archetypal beings early in my pagan path and they've continued to work with me since then, even though I'm a staunchly solitary practitioner.

So my path is very much an individual-based one. I've included some practices later in this book for potential group work with totems, such as a family or a coven. The one-on-one work is still important even in group situations, so it remains the main emphasis of this book.

How many do I get?

One of my great frustrations with nonindigenous totemism is the emphasis on prescriptive approaches. The whole "Everyone has X number of totems" idea is a good example. The value of X in that particular equation ranges from one totem (the monogamous solution!) to two (one on the left, one on the right) to four (one for each of the cardinal directions) or five (cardinals plus center). Sams and Carson, in their popular *Medicine Cards* system, came up with the number nine.[8]

I think there's no set number. Some people really do only have one totem they work with throughout their lives. Others may have a few or even a dozen. I have worked rituals and meditated with hundreds of totems in my life. Most of them don't have as strong a connection with me as Gray Wolf or Red Fox, but just as with our human relationships, totemic relationships vary as well. (I'll talk more about these relationships later.) Don't stress yourself out if you "only" have seven totems

---

8. *The Medicine Cards* (St. Martin's Press, 1999) are also a very good example of something to avoid in nonindigenous totemism—appropriation. Sams and Carson, among many other predominantly white authors, tout their work as "Native American." In actuality these works are usually mishmashes of random bits of lore taken from assorted indigenous American cultures and slapped together with some New Age material: *The Medicine Cards*, along with some vaguely racist content (choice quote: "All of our petroglyphs [in North America] speak of the Motherland, Mu, and the disaster that brought the red race to North America ...." (201) There's already enough misinformation about indigenous American cultures as it is without people making such inaccurate and hyperromanticized claims like that. If you want Native American spirituality, figure out which culture you're talking about and then find a way to talk to them directly, if they're open to it. (Okay, rant over.)

and you have no idea who the other two are, or if you've found nine and suddenly a tenth wants to say hi. You aren't trying to complete a checklist here.

Do they ever change?

Just as with human relationships, totems can come and go. Domestic Horse was a significant part of my life for a few years in my teens but didn't stay permanently. Conversely, Red Fox showed up in my twenties to help me through a tough period of my life and decided to stick around afterward. If a totem leaves, it doesn't mean that you're a horrible person or they hate you. It may be that they have nothing else to teach you, or they may have more pressing matters to deal with regarding their own children. I've included a ritual in chapter 5 to help ease the changes that may occur when a totem moves on.

Do I have to like my totems?

Some people assume that their favorite animal is their totem. While in some cases this may be true, you may also end up with totems that you never had a connection with before. You may even actively dislike some of them, especially the totem of an animal or other being you don't care for in everyday life.

I *hate* poison oak with a passion. I'm very sensitive to urushiol, the oil in poison oak and poison ivy that causes skin irritation and itching, so all it takes is me barely brushing by a plant to end up with a nasty rash. But I've had to come to respect the totem Poison Oak and its children because they're great teachers on boundaries and how to maintain them. Poison oak plants don't leap out and grab people but they do make sure no one tries to eat them, thereby preserving their leaves and other parts from damage.

Occasionally you may end up with a totem you fear, particularly an animal totem. An overly simplistic explanation often given in nonindigenous totemism is that it's a shadow totem, one that shows you your dark side and helps you come to terms with it. That's one possibility but as said elsewhere, I don't advise pigeonholing totems. A totem of a feared animal may be there to show you something entirely different or even ask you for help. Don't make assumptions based solely on your fear, but do take the opportunity to face your fear if you can, so you can see what's on the other side.

Are totems harmful?

Over the years I've heard stories of spiritual practitioners encountering hostile beings in their work. Sometimes these spirits attacked them during meditations; a few people claimed that the damage carried over into their physical lives. Admittedly I'm skeptical about these being anything other than internally-based psychosomatic responses rather than a "psychic attack" explanation. In any spiritual work I recommend that everyone keep a sharpened Occam's Razor in their kit—in other words, keep in mind that the simplest (and most mundane) answer is the most likely.

I have only rarely met with a truly hostile totem. One of the most notable examples was a number of years ago when I was exploring work with the totems of extinct species. I did a guided meditation to get in touch with Dodo, whose children were slaughtered by the thousands by European explorers in the 1700s until not a single one remained. When I approached the totem, it was sitting on top of a pile of dry and cracked dodo skulls, weeping bitterly. It attacked angrily when it saw me, chasing me off of its island. The sign was very clear: that particular totem wasn't in any mood to talk to me; however, I neither ended up with any physical effects, nor any string of bad luck in my waking life.

In cases where people feel as though a spiritual being has "cursed" them, I tend to figure that it's a case of confirmation bias—if you expect something bad to happen, then you're more likely to emphasize any negative occurrence in your life. Generally these can be traced back to perfectly normal courses of events and choices, and it's highly unlikely that anyone (spiritual or otherwise) is out to get you when you have that most human of experiences colloquially summed up as "s**t happens."

What methods can I use to find totems?

Some of us have it (relatively) easy in that we know at least one of our totems from an early age. Those who don't still have several options.

One of the most common methods people use is physical encounters with beings in nature. Perhaps they see an animal or plant that catches their eye, or they have an especially memorable experience climbing a mountain. In these moments of connection the totem reaches out to them. This does not, however, mean that every encounter in nature means a totem is afoot. My favorite example of this is red-tailed hawks. A person may see a hawk up on a phone line by their house every afternoon starting in spring. They may even think "Hmmm, what does that hawk mean?" What they don't consider is the fact that red-tailed hawks are territorial birds that migrate back to their homes in spring to breed, and that one pair works together to maintain their territory while they raise their young. Our yards make great hunting grounds for them to catch mice and other tasty rodents, and the phone line is a convenient perch. So for the most part all that hawk really "means" is that you have new avian neighbors raising their kids in your area. If you believe there's more to the story than that, I recommend guided meditation to ask the totem directly.

Dreams are related to nature sightings, except they occur when we're asleep. There are countless books chock full of stereotyped meanings for different things that appear in our dreams, like what it portends when a cow shows up in your dream.

The problem with this is that dreams are highly personal both in their symbolism and their content. Most dreams are simply our mind's way of filing away our waking experiences; our unconscious mind likes to speak in symbols and abstracts, hence how weird dreams can be to our waking selves. Most dreams don't have any particular significance beyond whatever we place upon them.

The other issue is that what a particular symbol "means" in a dream may vary from person to person. Let's look at a domestic dog, for example. To someone who loves dogs, that dream canine may be a portent of good news, companionship, or simply a happy memory of a childhood pet. To someone with a severe phobia of dogs, dreaming of a dog may be the onset of a terrifying nightmare. This is a rather extreme example, but just as totems don't have the same lessons and experiences for everyone, neither do dream symbols have specific meanings.

There are occasional dreams that seem too important to ignore, sometimes called "Big Dreams." They're the sort of dream you wake up from knowing that there was more to it, and can't shake it off once you're fully awake. If a Big Dream centers around an animal, plant, fungus, etc., it may be worth it to contact its totem to see if there was a message in there for you.

Another popular method is totem cards. These are decks of anywhere from about forty to eighty cards, similar to tarot cards, each one having a different sort of animal on it (less common are plants, fungi, and various other natural phenomena). You're supposed to shuffle the cards, pull out a certain number, and lay them on the table. Purportedly, this tells you who your totems are. The trouble, of course, is that there are a lot more than eighty totems out there. What happens if your totem is, say, Black Longspine Sea Urchin, but the only invertebrates in the deck you have access to are "Bee," "Butterfly," and "Spider"?

Most of these decks don't have cards for specific species.[9] Looking at our token invertebrates above, there are more than twenty thousand species of bee worldwide, twenty thousand

---

9. I have developed a thirty-four card deck that can be used to get in touch with the totem of any species of animal out there, not through specific species cards, but through more generalized traits like what continent the species is native to, what phylum it's a part of, and so on. The readings are interspersed with guided meditations, and while it's a more involved process than just laying out a few cards from an eighty-card deck, it's much more thorough and, in my experience, accurate. The deck is not available commercially, but I do explain how to make your own in my book *DIY Totemism: Your Personal Guide to Animal Totems* (Megalithica Books, 2008).

or so butterfly species, and thirty-five thousand species of spiders. Each species has its own behavior, habitat, and in some cases migration patterns. We think of bees living in colonies in hives, but many bees are solitary and live in burrows in the ground or old wood. And the lessons of a ground-hunting spider like Carolina Wolf Spider may be very different from those of a web-weaver like Australian Redback Spider, or the aquatic Diving Bell Spider, whose children live entirely underwater and carry a bubble of air with them as they go about their business.

The method I prefer is guided meditation. I'm not talking about a pre-written script where everything is already decided down to what the totem tells you. Rather, I use a more general set of directions with each meditation, enough to get you focused on the meditation at hand and then allowing you plenty of freedom to interact with the totems you encounter. When you do a guided meditation, you aren't going into the depths of the spirit world; the settings are in-between places partway between our world and that of the spirits. Proper journeying into the spirit world is a much more complicated and potentially risky business I won't be approaching for now.

Guided meditation also allows for more complex discussions than simply "What's my totem?" It's a great way to talk to your existing totems about things they need help with, and it's also an opportunity for totems you may not even have thought of contacting to reach you. In short, I prefer this method because of its flexibility and potential for deeper work. If you don't have a lot of experience with guided meditation, please see Appendix D for some helpful tips.

———

Allyson has been seeing a lot of fly agaric mushrooms lately. This fungus, with its well-known red cap and white spots, may be called a "toadstool," but she's more likely to see them with tiny insects crawling around them (no toads so far). The mushrooms have been popping up frequently in her wooded back yard, and she thinks she's seen more of them randomly in her everyday life on book covers, t-shirts, and even a greeting card at a nature shop. One night she has a dream about a giant fly agaric mushroom that towers over her home; there are other mushrooms of various types underneath it, but it's the one she notices the most. The next day she decides to contact the totem Fly Agaric to see if there's anything more to these odd occurrences. In her meditation she very quickly finds this fungus totem, again reaching high above her. It tells her that while it doesn't have anything for her, she should talk to the totem of the soil in her yard, which supports fly agaric as well as other fungus species. In speaking with Soil, Allyson finds out that some unhealthy influences have been introduced to the ground there. Once she comes out of the meditation, she finds her next door neighbor spraying their lawn with chemicals that drift over into her yard. They have a conversation about this, and the neighbor agrees to not spray within a certain distance of

Allyson's yard. That night, Allyson dreams of Fly Agaric
again, but this time the totem is small, the size of one of its
children, and Allyson feels a sense of contentment.

Why Work with Totems, Anyway?

If you've picked up this book it's likely that you're interested in totemism—but can you put a finger on why? I've already mentioned a few reasons for exploring this sort of nature-based spiritual path but I'd like to expand upon them a bit more.

Reconnecting with Nature

In the first chapter, I made the argument that most humans see themselves as separate from the rest of nature, an attitude that has had devastating effects on the environment and ourselves. As some of us seek to reconnect with our nonhuman neighbors, totems provide a "bridge" between us and the rest of the natural world. They are intermediaries between their species and everything else in the world, humans included. For that reason, they're already used to communicating with us and helping us better understand our nonhuman neighbors.

It's not always the most obvious totems who are spreading this message of reconnection either. One of my fungus totems is Black Mold. Mold is a pretty pernicious problem here in the damp Pacific Northwest, and I've had it crop up in bathrooms in more than one home I've lived in. I was pretty distressed when I saw it for the first time, and I knew it would be a couple of days before the landlord would be able to come in and clean the mold up. But even as I stared at the black spots on the ceiling, I felt a little nudge in my intuition and I allowed myself to pay attention to it.

Black Mold took the opportunity to remind me that just because I lived in a human-built shelter, it didn't mean I was separated from nature. It also helped me to be more mindful of the conditions I was living in; I had to adapt to bathrooms with poor ventilation and treat them a little differently than I was used to because of the increased moisture retention and decreased air flow. Just as animals that live outdoors need to care for their homes to keep them from becoming less effective, so too do I need to keep my own shelter in good working condition.

Totemism won't automatically make everyone more connected to nature. But those of us who do choose to incorporate totems into our spiritual practices often find we can't help but become reintegrated into the planetary dance of seasons and cycles. We rekindle our love for the world around us and act with more responsibility toward it.

The Power of Mythology

Humans are storytellers; we share lessons, ideas, and morals through our stories. The natural world has always provided us with a rich fabric for our stories, myths, and folklore. When we tell a story about an animal, the totem of that animal species then "includes" the tale in itself; the story becomes a part of it. Totems are then able to help us not only access that legend or myth but also to help us understand the animal behaviors and relationships that inspired the storyteller in the first place.

You can learn a lot about the contentious relationships many Europeans and their American descendants have had with wolves over the centuries by exploring the Big Bad Wolf. This caricature of *Canis lupus* may be found chasing pigs, goats, and even human children in stories from Germany, France, and elsewhere, and it has carried even further by modern media. The totem Gray Wolf has helped me to connect that character to the deep fear and misunderstanding about wolves that run in my culture's psyche and how it has negatively affected the very real, flesh-and-blood wolves that are now highly endangered in many places in the world.

Because they embody these stories and the natural history behind them, totems can also help us to write new myths about them and their children. For several years I've written myths about totems like Gray Wolf, Wolverine, Arctic Fox, and many others. I especially like writing about animals that have been unfairly maligned either because they're predators or are otherwise inconvenient for our needs. I meditate with the totems in mind and we write the story together; they inspire me and I choose the words. In this small way I try to change the way my culture views these misunderstood beings.

For Mutual Benefit

Most of the material available on totems promises us that we can gain lessons and tools from the totems all to help us change our lives for the better. While we shouldn't focus on that aspect exclusively, there's nothing wrong with asking for help.

When humans create rituals and other spiritual practices, we can call on totems (among other beings) to join us in these rites. Sometimes it's an invitation to a celebration where the goal is simply to enjoy each other's company and be happy about something good in the world. Other times we're asking the totems to help us with something, like a challenge we face or a lesson to be learned. Whenever I want to find a job or other work, I ask the totems American Badger and River Otter to help me out. I call on them in a ritual I do before starting my job hunt: I ask Badger to help me stay tenacious, strong, and patient; I ask Otter for help finding work I would enjoy and reminding me to take time out to play no matter what I'm doing.

It's not just about what we humans can get out of the bargain; totems do not exist only to impart great wisdom upon us. Their main concern is care for their physical counterparts, and an often-neglected part of totemic practice is asking how to give back to the totems and their children and doing what we can to help them. Several of my bioregional totems guided me to become more responsible for the land I live on and near, and part of that included adopting a stretch of the Columbia River shoreline north of Portland. Several times a year I pick up trash and other detritus and test the water for pollutants. Doing so helps animals that might otherwise mistake the litter for food, and it gives data to organizations that help keep the water from getting more polluted, which is good for every being that relies on the river.

"It Just Sounded Interesting"

Curiosity is a valid reason for stepping onto a particular spiritual path. Maybe an animal or other being showed up in a dream and you wondered whether it was a totem trying to get your attention. Or maybe you're in a stage of spiritual exploration and totemism is a subject that calls to you, even if you can't exactly say why. You might even have gotten this book as a gift and decided to give it a try for the heck of it. Whatever your way, don't think you have to leap in with both feet in order to be a genuine totemic practitioner.

———

Josie is recovering from a bad bout of depression. One of the exercises her therapist had her do was to make a list of parts of her life she felt like she'd let go of and wanted to return to. At the top of the list she writes "spirituality." She had gone to church with her family as a child, but now in her twenties she's interested in branching out a bit. She happens to pass by a metaphysical bookstore on her way home from work one day and decides to take a peek. She ends up buying a few books, including one on animal totems. She'd always liked animals but this is the first time she's thought of them being a part of her spiritual life. When she gets home, she curls up with her supper and the totemism book and begins to read...

There are plenty of other reasons you might like to work with totems. Perhaps you've already identified one or two totems that have made themselves known to you and you want to find out more about working with them. Or you might already be following a nature-based spiritual path and want to bring in totems to some of your practices. Your reasons are your own; you aren't limited to the ones I've mentioned here.

———

Now that I've introduced you to some of the totems, in the next chapter we'll take a closer look at how they're all connected and how to start creating relationships with them.

Four

The Totemic Ecosystem

Getting to know an individual totem can be a really rewarding experience; however, that experience is even more enriched when you also understand the connections it has to other totems, connections paralleled in the physical world. The animal totems I worked with insisted that I meet their nonanimal counterparts, and in doing so I was able to have more context for the lessons they were teaching me.

As one personal example, Steller's Jay made sure that the first time I went hiking in the Columbia River Gorge shortly after moving to Oregon, I was introduced to the totem Douglas Fir. Not that it was all that difficult to find it; it's one of the most common trees there. But Steller's Jay wanted me to know that Douglas Fir was incredibly important to them, because this tree is a common nesting site for jays and others. Douglas Fir, in turn, showed me how their physical counterparts were extraordinarily important for their ecosystems. Numerous animals, from Douglas squirrels to an assortment of tiny insects, as well as mosses, lichens, ferns, and other plants and fungi, all make their homes in living Douglas fir trees. When one of these mighty trees dies and falls to the forest floor, it becomes a nurse log—that is, a huge decaying hunk of wood that feeds countless living beings with its fibers and the nutrients therein. A tree sucks up a lot of resources in its lifetime, and when it dies, all those resources are released back into the ecosystem at large to be used by other beings.

As I got to know both Steller's Jay and Douglas Fir, they introduced me to even more totems in their ecosystem, and I became much more familiar not just with the ins and outs of the place and its inhabitants, but how the things I learned from each of them individually were also dependent on the teachings of the others. Why is this important to know? Well, why is it important to know a totem as well as its physical counterpart? The totems add a new dimension to the things we can learn from observing a place and its denizens. They embody patterns and connections, and they help us recognize why and how we can apply them to our own lives. Moreover, they familiarize us with our own part in the ecosystem, something that many humans have lost sight of. They are the ambassadors of their species, and the totemic ecosystem is the place where our physical world meets their spiritual one.

By spiritual, I don't necessarily mean "religious." Spiritual in this case merely means "not physical." What that means to you can vary; it could be an alternate reality that parallels ours, or a symbolic world created in our own creative minds. However, the totemic ecosystem is not entirely spiritual and therefore removed from this world. Just as totems are intermediaries between their species and ours, so the totemic ecosystem bridges their world and ours. Each ecosystem in the physical world has its totemic counterpart—I'll talk more in a minute about this concept.

Totemic ecosystems are not strange worlds of dreams where nothing seems to make sense. Instead, they mirror physical ecosystems, even looking much like the places themselves. The main difference is the totems themselves: while they may appear as an ordinary-looking animal, plant, etc., they may also manifest as much larger versions thereof. I've also had totems show up in anthropomorphic (partly human) forms as a way of demonstrating their ability to understand their own species as well as ours, particularly if they welcome contact from humans. No matter what, though, there's no doubt when they show up because they always put forth a sense of being much "bigger" and more powerful than an individual spirit.

They also may show up in their wild forms. A totemic ecosystem associated with a place that has been logged in the last century or two may reveal itself in a more ancient setting, what the land looked like before humans completely tore it to pieces. Some ecosystems may need to reach back much further, sometimes a millennium or more. Others may choose to take their modern form—a field of wheat or clearcut hillside, for example—even if it's not as pleasant as it was before. This may mean that depending on how a totemic ecosystem wishes to present itself, you may be talking to a vastly different array of totems than you were expecting. If your intent is to get in touch with its current incarnation, you may politely ask for that face in particular.

Boundaries and Parameters

So how big is a totemic ecosystem? The short answer is: it depends.

Have you ever walked into a meadow or patch of forest or stretch of desert and felt that it had a particular personality compared to the surrounding area? You've just sensed the totemic ecosystem. It can be as small as a little field or as large as the bioregion itself, and often a single spot may be the domain of several overlapping totemic ecosystems. In my own bioregion is a crossroads along one of my favorite places in the Columbia River Gorge, where trails 419 and 420 meet with a large Douglas fir tree and a few large stones in the center. It's partway up the mountain known as Devil's Rest and overlooks the Columbia River, with both Wahkeena Creek and Multnomah Creek—and the falls they both feed—close by. It's a richly diverse habitat typical of the Gorge with numerous species of animals, fungi, plants, and more. The trails carry energy from surrounding ecosystems, too.

With its tree and stones, this one crossroads happens to be at the center of where several totemic ecosystems meet. Now, how do I know that for sure? After all, the flora, fauna, and fungi around Wahkeena Creek are much the same as those along Multnomah Creek a mile or so away. Geographical features have longer lifespans than these, for the most part, and therefore they tend to contribute more influence to an eco-system. Additionally, they are largely responsible for what can and can't live in a place. The temperate forests on the west side of the Cascade Mountains couldn't grow on the east side be-cause the mountains create a rain shadow to the east, giving it a lot less rainfall and turning it into a desert.

Even west of the mountains the energy can be different on each side of the Columbia River. The land is primarily made of basalt from enormous volcanic flows that occurred about twenty million years ago in what is now Idaho. The Gorge it-self was created when a gigantic glacial lake near modern-day Missoula, Montana, repeatedly broke open between fifteen thousand and thirteen thousand years ago, each time sending a massive wall of water traveling up to eighty miles an hour all the way from Missoula to the Pacific Ocean (and in fact the current flowed a little way into the ocean!).

These repeated enormous floods cut into the ground, creat-ing the gorge. The basalt on the south side in Oregon is much more solid than that on the northern, Washington side, which tends to be more crumbly. This harder and more solid basalt doesn't erode as quickly from its many streams and the effects of precipitation and wind, so it has more sheer drop-offs. The waterfalls, in fact, are from streams that predated the floods; prior to the creation of the Gorge they would simply flow down the mountain slopes into the Columbia, but with all that land removed, they drop over the edge and continue their paths at much lower elevations. Across the river the land has eroded into a softer decline, leaving few drop-offs for falls to form over.

What's this brief geology lesson have to do with totemic ecosystems? Two sides of a river had very similar experiences in the past several thousand years—lava flows, giant floods, the same general weather patterns and climate, *but* the make-up of the geology makes them markedly different. Look at the rivers; the way a river flows gives it a sort of personality, and a waterfall has a different energy than a gently sloping stream meandering to its mouth. Moreover, the geology even affects what can live there; the south side of the Gorge is less protected from the weather systems that mostly come up from the southwest, drying the land out more. It also gets more sunlight, which bakes the very earth and contributes to its more crumbly nature. The animals, fungi, and plants living here must be able to deal with harsher conditions than their counterparts across the river.

As we've already established, the beings that inhabit the physical landscape and make up the landscape itself are the ones that determine which totems inhabit the local totemic ecosystem. That's why the totemic ecosystem feels a little different around Wahkeena Creek compared to Multnomah Creek; for the most part the denizens are the same, but each creek gives its own unique addition to its place, changing the overall feel in each.

That being said, you may end up in places in your meditations that don't seem to have physical counterparts. The realm of these meditations is less malleable than the purely spiritual world, but it's not as solid as our world, either. I have had paths that I know well in the physical world take strange turns in my meditations. Places have butted up against each other in meditation that in real life are miles away. This is usually a way for the meditation to take me to where I need to be much more quickly; for the most part, the land of meditation looks a lot like the physical reality.

Bioregions, Biomes, and Biotopes

It's perfectly acceptable if you happen to have trouble figuring out where the boundaries of a given totemic ecosystem are. What I've described so far is a fairly intuitive method of defining these boundaries. That's fine for some folks, but others tend to have strengths in other areas.

For some, the more concrete concepts of bioregions, biomes, and biotopes may be helpful. I've already talked about a *bioregion*, a particular area of land that has more or less the same physical features throughout it with more local variations (I'll talk more about those variations in a minute). A *biome* is a similarly large concept but is more defined by climate and the effects of things like average yearly rainfall and temperature fluctuations on the land and its inhabitants. Biomes are not limited to land; there are also aquatic biomes in both fresh and salt water.

The major difference is that a bioregion is a specific place, while a biome isn't just found in one location on the planet; the temperate steppe describes a variety of places ranging from the middle portion of Asia to part of eastern Australia. One bioregion that exemplifies the temperate steppe is the Great Plains of the United States; where it hasn't been plowed under for agriculture, it supports a rich grassland habitat with animals, plants, and other beings adapted to its semi-arid conditions and wide, flat or gently rolling layout, and sudden shifts in weather. While the individual life forms found in temperate steppes worldwide may vary, the general characteristics of climate and their effects are the same. There are several different competing systems for defining biomes; a good basic introduction can be found at http://eschooltoday.com/ecosystems /what-is-a-biome.html.

A bioregion describes a large place, and a biome describes the climactic nature of that place. A *biotope* is the corresponding microcosm, being a smaller part of the bioregion and biome. Synonymous with habitat, it is defined less by the geography and climate and more by the specific community of living beings populating it. Other parts of the biotope such as available water, weather, geology, and the like are seen as the home in which the animals, plants, and others live, but it is the uniformity of the living beings found there that ultimately defines the biotope. Biotopes are generally thought of as wilderness settings though there are urban biotopes as well, so don't think you have to go into the backcountry to do things right.

Biotopes may gently blend into one another, or they may be sharply defined. A good example is Forest Park in Portland; the park consists of more than five thousand acres of dense second-growth forest dominated by conifers. It is inhabited by a variety of animal species, from blue herons to coyotes to coastal cutthroat trout. As soon as you leave the park in any direction, you come across human development, especially at the southeast end which is firmly embedded in the city of Portland proper. Where the trails ends, the street begins, quite literally. Although there are efforts to restore some semblance of the original natural areas where the city now stands, the vast majority of species in Forest Park do not live in the urban parts of Portland; they are effectively distinct biotopes.

What makes the biotope different from the more intuitive totemic ecosystem? The totemic ecosystem—the "spirit" of a place—may not exactly overlap a biotope; you may sense a given totemic ecosystem's borders are smaller than those of the biotope it is in. This means that one individual biotope may include more than one totemic ecosystem, as in Wakheena and Multnomah above, which share the same biotope but are spiritually separate.

Totemic ecosystems may be larger than a given biotope, and indeed may nest within one another. As large as it may be, even an entire bioregion can encompass a totemic ecosystem in and of itself and have smaller distinct ones within its boundaries as well.[10] Sometimes we humans can be influential in the development of these systems as well. Oregon's borders are marked by certain natural features rather than just arbitrary lines drawn for geopolitical purposes. I can sense a difference any time I cross over the Columbia River into Washington or arrive in California after heading through the Siskiyou Mountains. But some of this may be influenced by the strong

---

10. During the writing of this book, I was trying to explain to other people what I was writing about. When it came to the overlapping nature of land and place totems, I described it as "the unholy love child of Russian nesting dolls and Venn diagrams."

identification many Oregonians have with their state; while we humans are far from the only species in this place, we do have a pretty significant impact on it, and a lot of people in Oregon in particular are invested in the land for its own sake.

Working with more clearly defined boundaries like biomes, biotopes, and even state and county lines can help you when trying to suss out the borders of a totemic ecosystem. Here's an exercise that may help you if the more intuitive boundaries seem a little nebulous. It'll take some investment of time and effort over a period of weeks or even months, but it'll give you plenty of practice in being able to notice unique totemic ecosystems.

First, identify a particular biotope near you that has reasonably well-defined boundaries to which you have access (no trespassing!). It may be a large city park, a particular system of hiking trails, or a rural nature preserve. It could even be the last remnants of farmland or forest left over from suburban sprawl. I generally recommend not starting with the biotope you live in if possible, since you're immersed in it all the time and are probably pretty acclimated to its feel already. You can always compare other biotopes to it later on, though.

Start at the edge of this biotope; if you can start on foot, so much the better, but other forms of transportation will work, too. Just be aware that the more complex a machine you're operating, the more distracted you may be from exploring the place you're in. If you can periodically find places to get off the bike or out of the car to walk or at least sit, so much the better. You may also wish to bring a journal, recorder, or other method of taking down your impressions after each part of the exercise.

As you venture into the biotope, clear your mind as best you can and notice how the place makes you feel. Do you feel comfortable here or intimidated? Welcome or unwelcome? Does the place feel happy, sad, or some other emotion? How physically accessible is it? Are there obvious trails (made by either humans or other animals) or is the landscape tangled and hard to navigate? What else immediately catches your attention about the place? Take at least a few minutes to explore the place in more detail as much as you're able. What stands out more as you spend more time there? How do you feel now that you've been there longer?

Now relocate to another part of the biotope. Ideally you'll be able to walk through it, though if you have to bike or drive in more deeply, do so. If you aren't able to go much further in, relocate to another place along the biotope's edge. As you move along, keep paying attention to how the place makes you feel and what you notice about it immediately, and then after you've been there a while. Keep taking notes as you go.

Once you've spent a fair amount of time in this biotope, you may start noticing its "personality." If not, that's okay. It can take a while, especially if you are new to this sort of intuitive work. Also, don't worry so much about listing off the animals, plants, waterways, and other features of the place. For now, you're just trying to get a general sense of it; we'll do more work with the details later.

In order to get a better basis for comparison, you'll want to repeat this exercise in at least one other biotope, preferably more. Try seeing what the difference is between your first biotope and another one of the same type of biome—maybe two different patches of temperate broadleaf forest. Then try comparing your experiences with those in a biotope of a different biome, like an arid desert or a large lake (especially if you can safely take a boat out on the water).

Ideally what will happen is that over time you'll start to notice that each place feels different from the rest. You might find yourself especially attracted to one biotope in particular; if so, spend more time getting to know its personality in more depth.

Keep in mind that other factors such as the weather, your mood, time restrictions, and the like may affect your perception of these places as well. Those factors are part of why it's important to return multiple times and see what you notice each time. It's also good to be aware of how things like cold, wet weather, or large crowds in public parks generally make you feel; if you go to a park that's really busy and you feel crowded and annoyed, that will probably affect your perceptions of the place. Also don't let other people's biases affect you. If one person says that a particular place creeps them out, don't feel deterred. The totemic ecosystem is a pretty subjective concept anyway, so it's most important to listen to your own intuition.

And if you just can't seem to get the hang of this intuitive approach, that's completely okay—it's not for everyone. Use the boundaries of the physical biomes and biotopes as your maps in working with the totems and their ecosystem and you'll be fine. You might even figure out your own methods of totemic work outside of what's described here; use whatever works.

———

James has always approached the world from a fairly analytical viewpoint. An engineer, his way of thinking has always kept him in good stead, and he enjoys learning the facts and measurements and other nuts and bolts of a given topic. Totemism is no different; while he enjoys being outside, he likes to prepare himself for hikes in new places by reading about them so he has more information to carry as he goes. When he starts working with the idea of a totemic ecosystem, he gravitates toward the concept of the biotope and decides to apply it to a new trail he's recently discovered but not yet hiked. He spends a couple of weeks researching the land where the trail is, how it was formed, what the climate is like, and what lives there. When he's able to hike the trail, he takes notes on what he finds there and how it matches his research. As he does so his comfort with the place increases, and he begins to feel that the little valley the quietest part of the trail goes through is especially significant—not just because it's the home for some very rare amphibian species, but also because it seems to have a life of its own. As he looks up at the ridge surrounding him, marking the clear lines of the valley, James quietly greets this place, and decides to dedicate himself to getting to know it better.

Studying the Totemic Ecosystem

Now that you've got some idea of where at least one totemic ecosystem is, it's time to get to know it in more detail. There are two primary ways to do this: research and experience. By now you've already dealt with both of these to at least a small degree. If you did the last exercise, you had to research places to go, how to get there, and where to go once you arrived. But you also experienced this place, at least a little bit.

These two methods of exploration should be considered complementary rather than contradictory. There's an unfortunate tendency among some spiritual people to claim that "book knowledge" is universally inferior to revealed theology, that belief is better than knowledge, and to apply pseudoscience as truth in places where science doesn't yet have an answer (or at least where no significant evidence has been found even through multiple experiments). These claims are no better than the ones of those who are so completely materialistic that they see no benefit whatsoever to creative human endeavors like storytelling and other attempts to make meaning of the world. At its best, spirituality brings us to wonder at the world around us, even if you don't take world myths and religions literally.

Bioregional totemism is a system that draws on research and experience alike. Totemic systems throughout history and around the world have been informed by the knowledge of the people that developed relationships with totems and ways of interacting with them. Direct observation has always been a central part of totemism; we as a species have learned from other animals, plants, and other beings, just by watching them.

We have access to an unprecedented amount of knowledge and information here in the twenty-first century. There are many more ways to observe the world from the tiniest particles to the universe our planet floats through. Microscopes and telescopes, chemistry sets and radio trackers, the Large Hadron Collider and all of NOAA's satellites—these and many more technological advances have helped us understand the natural world in all its parts to an extent never before seen. We can see bacteria and unicellular animals, plants, and fungi. We understand where in the universe the Earth is situated and why it revolves around the sun.

It's okay to have some subjective impressions as well; that's the basis of spirituality in general. Ancestral human observations were used equally for knowing when the deer were most active, when they were easiest to find, and for creating stories embodying feelings about watching the deer's strength and grace. Research helps us to keep our feet on the ground even as we have our heads in the clouds. Experience allows us the subjective wonder and joy at actually being in contact with things we may previously have only encountered in books.

With that in mind, revisit the questions I asked you about your bioregion in the "Hitting the Books" section of chapter 1, this time looking at one of the biotopes you explored (perhaps the one you liked best or connected with most strongly). You may have seen some animals there as well as native plants and fungi while you were visiting, and you probably noticed some other features of the area like landforms or water, natural or human-made. Take some time to do more research on the flora, fauna, and fungi of your biotope, in addition to its geology and geography, climate and rainfall, and other layers of the place. Explore the history of human habitation and other usage as far back as you're able. You can also look into any stories about the place whether that's indigenous myths and history or more recent occurrences and tales, all the way up to and including urban legends.

Spend more time at the place, too, experiencing and getting to know it, preferably on foot or sitting down. Make note of any impressions you have while there or anything that especially jumps out at you during your research to include living beings, weather patterns, and more. These may be absolutely nothing beyond your personal preferences and interests, but they might also become important as you're getting connected to the totemic ecosystem of this biotope.

That brings us to another layer of experience: spiritual practice. Spirituality isn't strictly about religion. Actually it is what helps us feel connected to and/or a part of something bigger than ourselves—and that "something bigger" can vary. Maybe it's a particular divine being, the planetary community, or even the universe itself. Why don't I present what's offered here as divine writ that must be strictly followed? In part, I know my readers come from a diverse set of spiritual backgrounds, and I'd rather you integrate the material here into your path as you see fit rather than try to shoehorn your way into my path.

The definition of "spiritual practice" as it relates to the totemic ecosystem may vary, though in this case the general goal is to feel connected in a spiritual sense to the biotope you're exploring. This may happen through something as simple as taking a walk through it, or sitting quietly and observing. Or you may wish to use meditation to get a "deeper" connection to the place and even start a conversation. Here's one you can use to start tapping into the spirit of a place and sensing its totemic ecosystem.

Find a relatively quiet place in your chosen biotope; bring a journal or other method of recording your results as well as a bit of protein-heavy food and some water. I recognize that some of you may prefer music or drumming to help you focus; however, I recommend avoiding those things here, as you want to listen to the sounds endemic to the place as much as possible, even if they come from people and cars. After all, we are a part of the landscape too, and if you're going to get a thorough understanding of the place, that includes the human element.

Sit, lie down, or otherwise make yourself comfortable there. Close your eyes if you like. Spend a few moments clearing your mind and focusing on the way your breath feels as it flows in through your nose and/or mouth, down into your lungs, and back out again. If someone walks by on a trail or is otherwise distracting, let them pass and keep focusing on your breathing and relaxation. In fact, if at any time you are distracted in your meditation, go back to the breathing and relaxation to calm yourself before returning to your meditation.

Next, open yourself up to what you feel and sense as you did when you were more actively walking around the place. Whereas before you were also paying attention to things you saw and heard and felt physically, now focus on your intuition, emotions, and instincts; your feel of the place. You might even imagine your energy intertwining with that of the place, being one animal among many here in this biotope. Spend at least a few moments connecting with this experience, longer if you like. In fact, you can make an entire meditation out of this part of the exercise alone.

If you want to try something different while still staying in touch with the spirit of the place, visualize how it looks without opening your eyes. Imagine the area directly around you, the little patch of ground you're resting on, the plants and rocks and other things within a few feet of you. Then expand that awareness a little further, maybe twenty feet away from you. Hold that awareness for a few minutes. It may look more or less like it does in the physical world, or you may find that parts of it are very different—some living beings may glow with a green or other colored light, or you may see animals there that weren't apparent in the physical world, or the weather may be different. You can make an entire meditation out of this exploration, too.

If you want to go a bit further, imagine you're walking or otherwise moving around this twenty-foot circle of land you're holding in your mind. See if the sensations you feel about the place shift as you explore. Do you feel a particularly strong pull toward a specific plant or animal? Do you find yourself wanting to look for water or wishing it might rain? Is there a path or place in the distance you want to explore more? Again, are there any significant differences between what you see in your visualization compared to how the place looks in the physical realm? Does your energy change at all as you explore?

If you feel comfortable, visualize yourself moving further out from that circle, wherever you feel drawn. Keep note of what you notice, what seems more apparent or interesting to you, and what makes this place different from the physical world, or whether they're basically the same. Keep attention also on your sense of the place, the energy it has, and what effect that energy may have on you. If you notice a place where the energy suddenly shifts in character like you've crossed over a boundary, note where that is. You might even try following the boundary to see where it goes.

When you're ready, return to the place you started; if you're having a little trouble finding your way back, just remember what the place looks like and you should be brought back there. If you're still a little lost, start wiggling your fingers and toes a bit—your body is still grounded in that starting place and that bit of movement should return you. Imagine your energy returning to your body, untangling from the place's energy. Start to move a little more keeping your eyes closed; maybe stretch a little bit, rotate your shoulders, and other small movements. Then open your eyes, eat a little food and drink some water, and take a few moments to ground yourself in your body and the physical world again before recording what you experienced in your meditation.

You can certainly do this exercise again either in the same place or at another spot; if you noticed a boundary, you might go over to where you noticed it and start exploring that place both physically and spiritually.

The various stages of this meditation are good for simply connecting with a place as well. Just as we like to spend time with our friends with no real goal other than the enjoyment of each other's company, it's nice to be able to do this with the places we like as well.

Whatever combination of study, physical exploration, and meditation you choose, try to be as thorough as you can in learning about this biotope with the resources at hand. You don't have to become the ultimate expert on a given biotope, but do give it your best. You might also find that your studies and explorations take you in other directions; maybe another biotope adjacent to the one you're studying catches your attention or you find out about another place that draws you in even more. Leave yourself open to whatever options come up, and don't try and overthink things. Learn, absorb, and see what happens from there.

Totemic Relationships

Now that you have a sense of the totems' ecosystem, the next step in this whole process is what most people first ask: how do you find *your* totems? Before we get to the act of searching, a brief word about what "your totems" really means.

In my years of talking with others about totemism, I've sometimes encountered the idea that everyone has a set number of totems. Some people say every person only has one for their entire lives, others say two for balance, four for the cardinal directions, or even nine! In my experience, there's no hard and fast limit in play here.

Consider the totemic ecosystem: while you may make a number of acquaintances in your study of a given place, you probably won't connect with every single totem represented there. That's okay—trust the ones you do connect with to help you find who and what you need at any given time (and when in doubt, ask).

Maybe you're wondering why you can't just collect a complete set. Think of relationships with totems as very similar to relationships with other spiritual beings—and indeed with beings in general, human included. Each relationship is its own entity, and just like you don't stamp your friends into a BINGO card to make sure you win at life, you don't need to try and acquire a certain totem for each direction, day of the week, and so forth. That being said, I've found three general categories into which relationships with totems may be sorted: primary, secondary, and tertiary.

- *Primary totems* are with you for your entire life, whether you know they're there or not. They can have a very strong influence on you, and people who have one or more primary totems often identify very deeply with them. Primary totems are what a lot of people think about when talking about one's totems. Gray Wolf is one of my primary totems; as I've talked about, this totem showed up when I was still very young and has been a strong influence on me ever since.

- *Secondary totems* enter our lives to help us through a particular period of time or teach us something new. They may bond very deeply with us during their work with us, but eventually the work is completed and they retreat from our lives, though they may drop in now and again to check in, and we can do the same. I was badly bullied throughout my childhood by my peers, and by junior high and high school it had gotten really awful. During those years, Gray Wolf stepped aside and let Domestic Horse take over. Horse showed me more about independence and creating an identity for myself, as well as giving me something to focus on besides my daily torment. Near the end of high school Horse said farewell, and Gray Wolf stepped in again. Horse and I still occasionally meet in passing in my meditations and such but we haven't had the same closeness we did in my teen years.

- *Tertiary totems* are ones we contact for help with specific problems or to invite into a particular ritual or sacred space. Our relationships with them are strictly situational, and we go our separate ways once the task is complete. I asked Wolverine for help writing a totemic myth a few years ago featuring that totem as the central character, and while it worked out beautifully, it's the only time we've ever worked together.

Don't think you have to use these categories religiously. I won't be referring to them much throughout the book, and I offer them more as a convenient organizational system to help you understand the relationships we have with totems can vary widely.

———

Asha has been working with her totems for almost a decade. Her primary totem, Yellow Houseplant Mushroom, appeared to her in her very first meditation; she'd seen the physical fungi in her container garden for years but the totem wanted to introduce itself more properly. It's taught her quite a lot over the years about taking opportunities as they arise and being content with what one has, both of which have helped her survive the sometimes lean economic conditions she has faced at times.

For a period of time, Swiss Cheese Vine, the totem of a tropical plant she was fond of, and whose pots seemed to be especially prone to mushroom outbreaks, acted as a secondary totem to Asha. It demonstrated the importance of interdependence with those around you, even if it isn't always easy, and helped her get through a period where she lived with some difficult roommates she couldn't afford to leave. While the totem itself moved on, Asha still keeps a few Swiss cheese vines in her houseplant collection.

At one point, her roommates' late work schedules were so disruptive to her sleep that prior to having a discussion with them about the problem, she called on the totem Amethyst in a ritual one night to help her sleep better as well as Moonstone for peace and confidence. These tertiary totems were able to offer their energy in the ritual

and conversation that ensued, but that was the extent of
her work with them.

Finding Your Bioregional Totems

Now we get to the part that almost everyone wants to jump to
first—figuring out who your totems are. There's a good reason
I spent the past three-and-a-half chapters talking about other
things: finding your totem is not some miraculous event that
suddenly answers all the questions you've had about "life, the
universe, and everything."[11] Actually, finding them opens up a
lot more questions, and having some context to work with can
help once the floodgates open.

So far, I've also been preparing you for the actual search
itself. I wrote earlier about a number of methods commonly
offered for discovering the identity of your totems like dreams,
animal sightings, and card decks with different creatures and
other beings on each card—but that's not what we're going to
be working with here. Instead, what I've been helping you do
is familiarize yourself with the home of the totems of a given
place, the totemic ecosystem. Why?

Familiarity with the land will always help you narrow down
the possible totems you can work with. Every single species of
living being, mineral, type of waterway, etc. has a corresponding totem—and that's a lot of totems, by the way. By connecting yourself to a given biotope and its totemic ecosystem, you've
significantly shrunk your options, which isn't a bad thing. The
process of finding a totem is less like picking out the perfect

---

11. From the incomparable Douglas Adams, of course.

greeting card and more like turning a radio dial until you find a live signal: you're not so much making a conscious choice as allowing the right connection to happen.

This method of finding a totem also serves as a good opportunity to get a feel for what exactly you have on the other end of the signal. Totems, as I mentioned, are great archetypal beings, not individual spirits. To me, the totem feels *bigger*. It's like the difference between walking in a field of dandelions and through a stand of tall redwood trees—the presence is simply *more*.

You'll have already done a lot of the groundwork necessary for working with your totems in a bioregional sense. As I mentioned earlier, many people have this idea that totems are disembodied beings floating around until someone calls on them. We know now this isn't so, and a lot of the deeper work of totemism involves being familiar with the natural history and other traits of the totem's physical counterparts and their habitat.

Bioregional totemism is ultimately about totemism for the purpose of connecting with the land and its denizens. It's not only about what you can get from the totems or what great wisdom they can impart upon you. It's about connections and relationships, and by showing the totems you've already learned something about their homes, you've demonstrated a certain amount of respect for what they hold dear.

You may be fortunate in that one or more totems native to your bioregion already made themselves known to you either during another exercise in this book, or even before you picked it up. In that case, you're welcome to start doing some of the continuing work here with them if they're open to it. If you don't yet know any totems, it's okay to be a little more proactive in making that first connection.

If we aren't using cards or dreams to find totems, what are we going to use? More guided meditation. In this case we won't be working with a completely prescribed exercise where the path is already laid out for you. Instead, it's a framework in which you can get into the right mindset for meeting totems and communicating with them to determine whether they'd like to work with you. What happens during the meditation will be determined by you and any totems you may meet.

The meditation provided here is based on a structure I've been using for more than a decade, itself inspired by structures used by other practitioners for even longer. The words may be unique, but the concept is more or less the same.[12] You're going to enter into the totems' realm, using the physical place you're at as your "home base," as it were.

Let's talk safety. People have asked me whether it's dangerous to go into the spirit realm at all, if animal totems could bite them or an angry mineral totem could curse them for accidentally kicking it. It's reasonable to be concerned, and you should be fine with common sense, respect, and care. The totemic ecosystem isn't very deep into the spirit realm; it's more of a halfway point between the spiritual and physical, so you're

---

12. If you'd like to read a little more about how and why guided meditations of this sort work, I wrote up a blog post about it a few years ago at http://therioshamanism.com/2011/10/11/deconstructing-the-totemic -guided-meditation/.

unlikely to get horribly lost or come back from your meditation feeling off-kilter. In nearly twenty years of totemic work,
both my own and observing others', I've yet to see a totem be
outright hostile and aggressive toward a person for no good
reason. This isn't to say totems don't ever get upset or angry,
but in my experience the worst they're likely to do (especially
in this sort of meditation), is kick you back into our world and
ignore you for a while (a long while, if need be). I haven't seen
any cases of angry totems cursing people or following them
around and wreaking havoc on their lives poltergeist-style.
Generally they have much bigger problems to deal with and
would rather spend their time focusing on who they know can
help them and will appreciate help in return than wasting time
on getting revenge and punishing the disrespectful.

   With that in mind, we continue to the meditation itself.

———

Go to the place in which you've been most comfortable as
you've been exploring your bioregion. (If you don't think you
know quite enough about it, spend a little more time researching and exploring it before attempting this meditation.) If for
whatever reason you're unable to go to that place, but you have
a little piece of it like a rock, stick, or even a picture of it, do
your meditation elsewhere with this symbolic item.[13] Find a
quiet place where you're not likely to be disturbed or at least
are out of the way of others.

---

13. The next chapter addresses ways to create a special object linked to this
    land without taking anything from it.

If you would prefer to have someone with you, make sure it's someone who understands what you're doing and that you just want them to sit quietly with you to make sure nothing happens to you while you're focusing on the meditation, and to make sure you eat and drink and ground once you're done. While you're meditating, the person is free to engage in some other quiet activity like drawing or reading nearby.

As before, make yourself comfortable and spend a few moments relaxing and focusing on your breathing, preferably with your eyes closed. Visualize the place you're in, and feel yourself connect to it as you did before. Imagine your energy again weaving into the energy of the place, being one animal among many here. Through that energy, send out a call to the totems, announcing that you're ready to learn more about them and their home and that you're asking for a guide. You might even think something specific, like the following:

Beings of this place, guardians over those who grow and breathe, who flow and form, the solid earth beneath me and the air around me, who formed this place and inhabit this place: I am here with you.

Beings of this place, I have learned what I can of your home, from the knowledge of my people to what I have brought with my own senses physical and spiritual alike.

Beings of this place, I want to be more a part of it instead of merely walking on it; to remember who I am as a human animal and to be an ally to you and your kin.

Beings of this place, I need your help to do this, to learn and connect more, to be more aware and responsible, to be a better part of this community and give back to it for what I have been given.

Beings of this place, I ask for your help and for a guide.

Pause for a moment, and let this intention move outward from you. Then imagine walking or otherwise moving deeper into wherever you are. If you feel drawn in a specific direction, head that way. Be aware of anything that stands out to you—a particular landform or waterway; a fungus, plant, or animal and so on.

Ideally, a totem will make itself known to you. An animal totem may walk up to you, or a plant or stream may call out to you or shine with a bright light. You may feel especially drawn to a stone or rocky outcropping and start the conversation when you arrive. However it happens, it will be apparent that the totem is making an overture to you. Greet it and thank it for its time, then ask it why it has called to you. Let the conversation flow naturally; this is only your introduction. Take as much time as you like, too; there's no deadline.

If you aren't sure what to ask, here are a few potential questions:

- Why did you come to join me here?
- What makes this place special to you?

- What do you think are some of the most important things to know about this place?
- What can I do to help you and your children (physical counterparts) in this place?
- Are there other totems it might be good for me to talk to?

With regards to that last question, the totem you're talking to may indeed introduce you to others in this meditation or recommend some to contact at another time. Even if not, you've made a good first introduction. When you and the totem are done talking, thank it for its time and then start heading back to where you began the meditation, again taking note of anything that catches your attention or seems out of the ordinary.

Resume movement slowly, starting with your fingers and toes. Do some stretching and open your eyes when you're ready. As soon as possible afterward, record everything you can about the meditation; describing it to your companion may help as well.

Not everyone gets "perfect" results the first time, and that's okay. Maybe a totem didn't make contact with you or you might have been unsure if you were getting a signal. Sometimes a flash of wing from an unknown bird or a particularly shiny stone can be invitations from totems, but they can also be simply going about their business. If you aren't sure, give yourself a few days to recover and then try the meditation again, this time specifically asking for that totem to please come speak with you. If they make themselves known, ask whether your first sighting was incidental or they were trying to get in touch with you.

If you didn't get anything special the first time around or you had trouble staying focused on the meditation, don't worry. It happens to lots of people, especially those who are new to guided meditation and visualization. Usually what helps is more practice. Or it may be that no totem from that place feels ready to work with you just yet, in which case you have a couple of options: keep spending time there to see if one eventually makes itself known, or try in another location. (Or you can do both, if you want to hedge your bets!)

Also, it's possible you may be overlooking a totem. It's easy for us to get really focused on the more obvious ones like animal and plant totems and particularly the big impressive ones like wolves and eagles and big, tall trees. The one you may really need to talk to, though, may be the totem of the soil itself, or a fungus living inside a dead log, or a tiny little spring hidden in the woods. And once we get further away from our own animal kin, the ways in which the totems communicate and see the world may seem quite alien to us, so we might not recognize it at first. Remember the multi-layered nature of land totems too. If you're speaking to the totem of Soil, you may also find yourself talking with several fungus and mineral totems, which is why it's important to leave yourself open to whatever may happen.

Zach has spent the past couple of months getting to know a particular desert plateau near his home, doing research and hiking a couple of times a month to its top and exploring up there as well. He enjoys meditating next to a particularly large piece of sandstone shaped a little like a heart on its side. Mixed in with the sand are bits and pieces of other types of stone, something that's always fascinated him. When he does his meditation to find a totem here, the totem Sandstone almost immediately grabs his attention. Sandstone tells Zach about the history of this place, how the stone itself was made of sediment laid down almost 250 million years ago, and the little pieces of other rocks were eroded remnants of the Ancestral Rocky Mountains that were created over 300 million years ago. Then Sandstone introduces Zach to other land totems, including Mountain and Wind Erosion, both of which have had a significant impact on this one piece of sandstone and the plateau as a whole. While Zach already knew the facts about this place, having these totems play out the story in his meditation makes it even more vivid, and it helps him further appreciate the dry beauty of the land here. Over time, Sandstone introduces him to other totems in the area, but Zach always maintains an especially fondness for those of the physical land itself.

Where To Next?

Once you've met your first bioregional totem, you have a couple of options on where you can go, assuming a clear path hasn't already been indicated to you. You can ask the totem to introduce you to others if they haven't already, or you can make a deeper study just of that one totem. Both of these will ultimately familiarize you more deeply with the biotope and corresponding totemic ecosystem you're exploring, just from different angles. Do be aware that your first bioregional totem may have suggestions on which method is better for you; you may wish to go out and meet all the totems you can, but your first may recommend you work more deeply with it for a while before branching out to others. It's best to listen to them unless you have a really compelling reason to do otherwise; they may have particular ways in which they want to teach you things or at least help you get more prepared for totemic work in general.

Yearlong Study, Party of One

Some people work best by having a single focus as an anchor and selectively moving out from there. If this describes you, one thing you may wish to consider is doing a year-long study of your initial bioregional totem (the one you have the strongest, best relationship with) and its physical counterparts.[14] This will allow you to observe their place in the ecosystem throughout the seasons.

This exercise is similar to one I outlined in my earlier book, *Plant and Fungus Totems,* but broader and more focused on totemic relationships. Choose a location you can get to on a regular basis, at least once a month (more if possible) and in which

---

14. Note that I didn't say "primary" here, but "initial" or "first" instead. Just because a totem is the first one to approach you doesn't mean it'll be a primary, as described earlier.

you can find physical counterparts of your first bioregional totem. If your initial bioregional totem is Brown Trout, pick a lake where the trout live, or a stream or river where they travel to spawn even if they don't inhabit that stream or river much of the year. Your goal is to understand the importance of that place to the totem and its species/type, as well as its interconnection with other beings and phenomena there. Make sure you take notes so you can compare them from month to month.

Try to go in a variety of weather conditions, not just when it's sunny; if you can safely be there at night, try to do a couple of visits in the dark, too. Dress for the weather and be prepared to retreat to safety if the weather turns foul or you feel unsafe otherwise. You want to try to get a realistic perspective on what your totem's children experience throughout the year, but not at the expense of your own health.

When you first arrive for a visit, see if you can find a physical representative of your totem. If your totem is a land totem, like a mineral or natural force, this may be pretty easy. An animal totem may make things more challenging; you may only find signs it's been there, like prints or scat or shed skin. Still, do your best to make initial contact, if possible. Even if it doesn't happen when you first get there, you may run into them later on in your visit.

Think some about the research you've already done about this place and perhaps some other questions you may have about it. What's the history of your totem's species or phenomenon in this place? How long has the species been living here? In the case of a land totem, when was its physical counterpart formed, and how has it changed since then? How have humans affected it both in the past and present?

Next, start exploring the area and notice how it may have changed since your last visit. How are the plants and fungi? How wet is the soil, and how high is the level of any nearby waterway? Is there any noticeable erosion of stones or other landforms? Is the temperature different? What's the weather been like? Has there been an increase or decrease in human activity or development? What else do you notice about the place?

Now look at these same features from the perspective of your totem's children. What are the most important things about this place to them? If you're working with a biological totem, such as of a fungus or a plant, what do the plants or fungi need to survive and thrive here, and what threatens them? If you have a land totem instead, perhaps personified here as a rock formation or spring, are they at any risk of destruction through human or other means? What other beings rely on them, be they food, shelter, or other resources? What might be affected if your totem's physical counterparts were no longer here? Try to map out all these interconnections just within the immediate place you are, perhaps within a hundred-yard radius.

Take some time to meditate with your totem here in this place. It's a good opportunity to check in with it not only about what you've been learning, but also to ask what you can do to help, particularly if the place or its inhabitants are threatened in any way. And if you've been wanting to do any rituals with the totem (more about that in the next chapter) you can take advantage of their physical proximity here.

It's also fine to spend some time simply relaxing, whether hiking, having a picnic, or sitting and enjoying the day. You're welcome to share this activity with other people so long as you're allowed some time for your individual spiritual work. While you're out, pick up any garbage you may find. If you see any new graffiti or a source of pollution, contact whoever manages the place, whether that's a park service, private owners, etc.

Once you're back home, take some time to review this month's results with previous visits. What differences have you noticed, and what's remained more or less the same? If your totem is a land totem, these factors may still be important to the beings that rely on its physical counterpart. After the first year is done, you'll have a pretty good picture of what your totem's "calendar" is like; it's something you may wish to incorporate into the sort of ritual work I'll be talking about in the next chapter.

Even after the initial year is up, you can still keep visiting the place and taking notes; it's just a good idea to get at least one full cycle of seasons in so you can see how the relationships shift and change as the year rolls on. Moreover, if you keep this up over several years you may notice some larger trends—for example, what happens if your area is hit by a drought, or especially cold weather? How do your totem's children and other parts of that place respond compared with other years? What adaptations have they made to get through these changes? You could potentially make a lifelong study of this one place and learn quite a bit from it.

You're going to get a much better idea of your totem's relationship to this place over time as well as how its physical counterparts are integral to it. It'll also help you better understand why your totem may be trying to teach you particular things and why those lessons are important to both of you.

———

Val's first bioregional totem is Pond; the biotope she has connected most strongly with has a kettle pond at its center, created by glacial activity thousands of years ago. Each month on the day (or sometimes evening) of the full moon, she visits this pond, sitting by its shoreline and watching the activity around it. She makes note of the various living beings that make this pond and its surrounding woods a home, and she notices how the waterline recedes as summer carries on, then refills with autumn rains. On clear days she can see the bottom of the shallow pond, and she wonders how many of the stones that lay beneath the water were left there by glaciers. On a particularly cold day in November, she imagines what this place must have looked like with hundreds, if not thousands, of feet of ice over it right where she sits. Each time she meditates with Pond, telling the totem her observations and listening as Pond gives her ideas for further exploration. To mark the completion of a successful year, Val invites a small group of friends to this special place and tells them about all she's learned. She also talks about how the pond is threatened by development nearby as well as garbage from other visitors. They decide to contact a local environmental nonprofit about how they can better protect the pond and its inhabitants, and as they leave to start on this task, Val silently sends a quiet prayer to Pond asking for help in this new endeavor.

Social Butterfly Totem

Others may wish to branch out immediately, making several totemic acquaintances, as it were. For those of you who prefer this strategy, you're going to be not only looking at the other totems connected to that first one you met in your meditation/ etc., but you're going to more actively work with them rather than having your initial totem as your main point of contact.

You'll probably find that these connections happen pretty organically. If your initial totem is of an herbivorous animal, it's easy to see their relationships with the totems of the plants and fungi the animals eat, and of the landforms that give them water and shelter. That doesn't mean you'll be best buddies with every single one of these totems; some may be very interested in meeting you, while others may be indifferent. If the latter ends up being your case, don't try to force the issue; let them be unless they decide to approach you later, or unless another totem more formally introduces you to them.

Assuming other totems haven't already approached you, the best way to get started with this is to ask your initial totem for suggestions. You might ask which ones are the most important to them or which they think are the best ones for you to meet. Ask if they're willing to make introductions for you; you can also use the guided meditation to go talk to these other totems yourself.

If you want to be a little more methodical about it, you might try starting with totems that have specific types of interdependencies with your initial totem, such as totems whose counterparts rely on each other for food or shelter. If your initial totem is Cave, you could start with the totems of all the living beings that use caves in your bioregion as shelter and places to find food. You might then move deeper into the caves and meet with Stalactite and Stalagmite, as well as Condensation, and the totems of Limestone and other minerals found there. Don't be concerned if other totems outside of this structure approach you in the meantime; work with them along with the rest.

———

Cherie is new to totemism but has already taken to it like the proverbial duck to water. For her, it's opened up an entirely new way to look at the world around her, a world she admittedly had taken somewhat for granted. So when she meets Sandhill Crane, her first bioregional totem in guided meditation, she's eager to "meet the whole family" as it were. She asks Sandhill Crane to introduce her to other totems in the bioregion that may be worth meeting. Over the next several months, Sandhill Crane introduces her to the totems of some species of animals and plants cranes feed on in addition to the water and other land totems that protect the places in Florida where Cherie's nearest population of sandhill cranes live. She also spends time near waterways where the cranes themselves may be found, studying their habitats and watching their behavior when they're nearby. In this way she gains a greater understanding of this special place and her own connection to it.

Somewhere in the Middle

You don't have to stick to one or the other of these methods religiously. It's common for people who do a yearlong study with one totem to also make connections with others over that time. However, they may not pursue these relationships as vigorously as the totemic social butterfly. Conversely, if you've been making the effort to try and make acquaintances with all the totems in a given ecosystem, you may find that there's one you especially feel drawn to, perhaps even more than the first one you met. That may be the one that helps you into a deeper understanding of the totemic ecosystem, the corresponding biotope, and the lessons to be learned from it.

What's most important is that you go at your own pace. There's not much point to a spiritual practice if it makes you utterly miserable and you aren't getting anything out of it. There's something to be said for challenges but not if they're counterproductive. So if you find something's just not working for you, step back and figure out what's causing the problem. Examine your options and change as needed.

What Do You Mean By "Work With?"

Throughout this book, I talk about "working with" totems. What does that mean exactly? Here are a few ways I've worked with mine over the years:

- Spending time learning as much as I can about them and their children as well as adopting some of their behaviors and traits to better understand them and to improve my own life.

- Regular conversations with them through meditation and other means, so I may learn more from them, answer any needs they may have of me, and in many cases simply enjoy each other's company.

- Spending time in the places where the totems may be found, not necessarily for any deep spiritual work but simply visiting for its own sake. Some of my most formative spiritual experiences have occurred when hiking or camping.

- Creating small shrines and other sacred spaces in my home for the totems to "live" in, sort of like spiritual guest rooms. This is a way to demonstrate their importance in my life and show them that they're always welcome here.

- Performing rituals for a variety of purposes: honoring the totems and thanking them for their help, celebrating nature in general or of a specific place, working magic on behalf of the totems and their physical counterparts, asking the totems for healing or other energy when I need it, and mourning the loss of sacred spaces or species destroyed.[15]

———

In the next chapter, I'll go into more detail into some of these practices.

---

15. While I do include a small number of rituals in this book, for the most part I am leaving it up to you to create your own. If you don't have a lot of experience with ritual work, I highly recommend Elizabeth Barrette's book *Composing Magic: How To Create Magical Spells, Rituals, Blessings, Chants, and Prayers.*

Five

Practices for the Totems and Yourself

Knowing your totems and how the totemic ecosystem is woven together is important in and of itself. And there's a lot more you can do with your totems beyond learning about them, their homes, and kin. They can be active participants in your life spiritually and otherwise, and this chapter focuses on some ways to invite them in further.

The practices in this chapter are divided into three categories. Practices of Place strengthen and focus the bond shared with the land and its energy. Practices of Action are designed to create active change in you and the world around you. Practices of Celebration offer you ways to show gratitude and honor to the totems alone and with other people.

Practices of Place

Just as we spend time with people we love to strengthen our relationships, so can we also dedicate practices to places to solidify our bond with them. The following practices are designed to help you gain some "quality time" with your bioregion. Try them out and see which ones work for you, and maybe even come up with some of your own!

The Altar of Curiosities

In the last chapter I mentioned setting up special places in the home set aside for the totems. One possible setup is an altar of curiosities. Inspired by the classic *wunderkammer*, or cabinet of curiosities, this altar is more like a personal museum in which various artifacts of natural history ranging from bones and feathers to plant and fungus samples to rocks and bottles of water are displayed. The original wunderkammer was a product of the Renaissance interest in nature and new scientific approaches to exploring the world; the altar of curiosities takes that concept and adds a spiritual component. Instead of just trying to have the weirdest, most exotic collection of curiosities, the altar is meant to be a microcosm of your bioregion.

You don't need a lot of items to make this happen. Remember that piece of obsidian I mentioned earlier in the book? It's connected not only to Obsidian and Volcano and Silica but also to the area it was born (and if it was moved to a new place later on, there as well). By extension, it also carries energy from the other totems associated with that place, even those not directly involved in its creation. When you take a piece of an ecosystem, you carry a bit of the entire thing with you.

All you really need are some items that represent different parts of your bioregion and a place to display them. Beyond that, it's entirely up to you, your creativity...and available space. The original cabinet was more of what we would consider an entire room, but these days even a small wall shelf will suffice if it's all you have. Here are a few ideas to get started:

- Collect a small stone or other item from every place in your bioregion that you've done totemic work at, or that you've otherwise felt a strong connection to. You can put the date you first visited each place on the memento you collect as a sort of story of your explorations. (This method works great for power spots as described later in this chapter.)

- Start a collection that represents the different biomes and habitats represented in your bioregion; as one possibility, I might have a small vial of water from the Columbia River for the freshwater habitat there along with a bit of sand from the bank to represent the unique habitat in the riparian zone, and a Douglas fir cone from a conifer-dominated forest next to dried leaves from an apple tree growing in the agricultural fields around Mt. Hood.

- Start with one totem in particular, such as the first totem you met, and build up a cabinet around it and the connections it has with other totems. (Be careful—this one can expand very quickly if you let it get away from you!)

- Have several cabinets, one dedicated to a different sort of totem. You might have one with samples of waterways all

over the bioregion, another representing the animal totems you've worked with, and a third depicting the forces
that shaped the land, from igneous rocks to tree limbs
warped by constant strong wind.

- Dedicate your cabinet to the totems you've worked with
and make it a home for them to come visit you any time.
Even if you have some that eventually part ways with you
like secondaries, you can leave their symbol in the collection as a memory of their time with you, or create a
separate space just for these memories.

When you're collecting items, make sure it's legal to do so.
Most state and federal parks as well as many city parks won't
allow people to take found natural or archeological items with
them. Check the gift shop to see if anything is available for
you to legally buy; as an extra bonus, the money will go to
help maintain the park. Otherwise you may ask a private land-
owner if it's okay to collect items in their yard or on their land.
Also be aware that some animal parts in particular are illegal
to possess; many people are surprised to learn that all parts
of most wild birds in the United States—to include naturally
molted feathers, egg shells, and empty nests—are illegal to
possess due to the Migratory Bird Treaty Act. You can find out
more about laws governing the trade and possession of animal
parts at http://www.thegreenwolf.com/animal-parts-laws.

You also have the option to buy some items online. It's not
quite the same as finding them yourself, but it may be better
than nothing if it's your only option. If you're of an artistic

persuasion, you can create images, statues, and other depictions of the totems; in fact, the cabinet of curiosities sometimes also held works of art and cultural items along with natural treasures. So if the parts and other remnants of a given animal, plant, or fungus are not legal to possess where you are, reproductions made from legal animal parts (such as domestic goose feathers painted to look like eagle feathers) or artificial stand-ins (like fake fungi made from polymer clay) will work just fine. The totems generally appreciate efforts to protect their children and will not fuss if the actual feather/branch/ etc. is not used to represent them.

Speaking of cultural items, some people may wish to include representations of a place's indigenous people to create a full picture of that location's history. Because some cultural artifacts have been taken from their homes illegally, even by force, I recommend avoiding these unless you are very sure of their ethical origins. If the indigenous people are still around, a good option could be buying art an indigenous artist has made. If the culture no longer exists, look for a good-quality reproduction of an ancient artifact; it will probably be more affordable, and you can avoid the potential issue of buying something that was illegally stolen from an archeological site or museum or from the people while they still lived.

———

Gretchen is a natural history museum curator who has her own collection of personal treasures. She especially enjoys collecting items from her local area and likes to show them to friends and family who visit her at home. One set of shelves is particularly special to her: her altar of curiosities. It's tucked away in her bedroom where she has more privacy, and only a few people have been allowed to see what she keeps there. For several years she's been working with totems of her bioregion, and her altar representing them has grown along with her spirituality. While most of her collection is original specimens and artifacts including some antiques, she does have a few reproductions like resin bird skulls and a small but intricately detailed oil painting depicting people who lived in this area around ten thousand years ago. While not all of them may be museum-quality, each one has a story to tell and a special place in her spiritual practice.

Grounding in Gravity

Gravity is ubiquitous. The earth exerts gravity on everything on its surface as well as the moon and all the human-made satellites orbiting the planet. The sun, in turn, uses gravity to keep the planets and asteroids in their elliptical dances. Even we exert tiny bits of gravity on each other—it's not enough to make a real difference, but it's enough for the romantic notion that we really are attracted to other people.[16]

---

16. In other words, we do have a gravitational field, just like any other object that has mass. However, our gravity is so weak that we have no effect on the curvature of space, so in effect our gravity is more a curious side effect of us having mass than any sort of cosmic superpower. We can still dream, though, to include living vicariously through the Marvel Comics character named Gravity, who can indeed use his body's gravitational field to affect the world around him.

Gravity also isn't going away. No matter what we do, the huge mass of the earth will keep us in place, and it is only through immense effort and technology that a few of us have been able to break free of its bonds for a little while. This consistent force can be frustrating for those who wish to fly without wings or travel to the moon with the ease of taking a crosstown bus, but it can also be comforting.

One of the first things many people learn in meditation and other spiritual practices is the concept of grounding. Grounding (or earthing) is the act of feeling connected to something bigger than yourself and allowing that to help you feel calmer and safer. That "something bigger" may be the earth itself, the memory of a safe place, or the idea that things happen for a reason. You can also think of it as being similar to electrical grounding, which is where the term likely originated. As it relates to how electricity is used in household three-prong outlets, some plugs connect to a ground wire via a third prong that allows excess voltage to drain harmlessly into the earth. The ground wire prevents electrical overflow into an uninsulated piece of metal or exposed part of whatever is plugged into the outlet, which could cause a fire or shock whoever touches it. In spiritual or energetic grounding, you're plugging yourself into the earth itself, letting it take on any excess or frayed energy. The process gives you something to help bring yourself and your energy back into focus and control.

There are numerous techniques for grounding that involve the earth itself, but I quite like gravity in particular. It holds us close and safe and keeps our atmosphere from flying off into space—things I appreciate a lot! So I also enjoy grounding into gravity whenever I feel like I'm losing control of things.

Gravity itself is a pretty impersonal force dependant on mass, not personality. Here I'll explain how you can ask its overarching totem, Gravity—whose bailiwick includes both the earth's gravity and your own—for help in gravitational grounding. It's a great way to calm yourself in a moment's time, even when things are going crazy around you.

Get yourself into a quiet place if possible, though this exercise can be done anywhere, even in the middle of chaos. Wherever you do it, make sure you're physically safe before stopping for a moment to do it.

Take a moment to slow your breathing and close your eyes. Now focus on the weight of your body on the ground, floor, or whatever surface you're on. Feel the force of gravity pulling you downward, constant and strong. Feel it cradle and envelop you, as it does for everything on the planet. Also feel the gravity inside you pulling ever so slightly against the earth, completing the cycle.

Say or think the following:

Totem of Gravity, watcher of this force that binds us all together, let my energy be pulled into the earth's into one pure flow. Let loose strands come together, let the ruffled feathers be smooth, let the scattered stones return to the path.

Feel as the gravitational force holds you as one singular being, wrapping up even your gravity into its embrace. Let Gravity the totem guide your frayed ends back into a singular focus, and feel yourself become calm once again.

After enough practice you may not even need the little prayer in there; all you may need is to focus on gravity's effects for a moment, and let that be enough to pull you together. This can be really helpful in a tense situation where you don't have time to walk away but you need to stay focused on the task at hand. After all, gravity is all around us, as is its totem, so help is never far away.

Power Spots

Power spots are places on the earth that have a particularly strong presence to them, or otherwise seem special. For some people, such locations are limited to places with a lot of cultural significance (and often amazing feats of architecture) like Stonehenge and the Egyptian and Mayan pyramids. Other people believe invisible lines of energy called ley lines crisscross the earth and where they meet, power spots occur.

I'm not going to talk about monuments here. While these places may indeed have a great presence to them, due no doubt to their popularity as spiritual tourist destinations as much as their ancient significance, they may not have any real personal significance. It's like comparing an American Catholic's visit to the Sistine Chapel with his or her own church at home; the former may be a moving experience, but there isn't the same long-term relationship as there is with the congregation met in worship each week.

The significance of long-term spiritual relationships is the same with us nature-flavored folk. If you want to take a trip to

Stonehenge, by all means take the opportunity; I've heard it's pretty impressive in person. Taking time to identify some of your own power spots, those places you find rejuvenating and especially sacred is just as important.

So what makes a place a power spot? The matter is largely subjective; all places have their own power of one sort of another; we choose to acknowledge some places over others as being more sacred, meaningful, or re-energizing to us. Here are some things to think about when you're considering the places you've been as potential power spots:

- What places make you feel especially energized after you've been in them a while? Whenever you're stressed or going through a tough time, where's the place to which you feel the most drawn?

- Where are the best places to connect with your totems? Where have you had especially profound experiences with them? Do any seem to have been especially conducive to meditations, rituals, and other such practices?

- Of the people you know, has anyone identified any places as particularly strong or special? You might try visiting those spots to see how they feel to you. Don't just go on what they say; trust your own judgment. A place that is sacred to one person may not speak to you, while your most sacred site may perplex others.

- Any places that stand out physically such as rocky outcroppings, bodies of water, or even locations with large, old trees may be powerful places. In the Pacific Northwest, there's not a lot of truly virgin old-growth forest left. The patches that remain carry an incredibly primeval energy, remnants of something almost lost. If you can make a healthy connection with them, they can be wonderful power spots.

- Sometimes the places where we spend the most time come to share power with us. I adopted my beach along the Columbia River in 2012 and my main intention was to do the required cleaning and quarterly reports on the condition of the land and water. However, as I continued to care for the place, it began to open up to me. In the spring of 2014, it showed me a particularly secluded little trail I hadn't been on before, and took that opportunity to open up to me in a way it hadn't before. It is still a place with much healing left to do, victim of a lot of littering and other pollution, more than I can possibly handle myself. But because I cared enough to at least try and make it better, it gave me a bit of itself in return. Are there any places like that for you? [17]

If you aren't sure whether a place is a power spot, the best way to know for sure is to visit it and allow yourself to be open to it. Let your intuition guide you, and ask your totems for

---

17. In case it needs to be said, don't just start cleaning a place up in the hopes it'll give you great power. Offerings to places like this should be done without expectation, and for the purpose of giving service to the land. If you are fortunate enough to have the place give something in gratitude, treat it like a very rare, personal gift.

help, too. You might try meditating in the place (or at least sitting quietly and letting yourself feel whatever emotions and sensations arise there) and see if it feels stronger or otherwise different from the surrounding area. Or you might go visit your totems through guided meditation and ask them to lead you to a power spot. Some people get the best "feel" for a place with bare skin, so if it's safe and comfortable for you to walk barefoot or otherwise touch the land with your bare skin, let that be an additional taste of its energy.

Another possibility is divination. I'm not as fond of it in this case because I prefer a more direct, feet-on-the-earth approach. Some find it a good focus for their intuition, so it may work for them. There are a number of divination methods you can use—a pendulum, casting bones, even a specially made dowsing rod—but the end result should still be a tool that indicates where in relation to you a power spot is located. You could ask the pendulum to swing in the direction of where a power spot may be found. Of course, given the fact that a pendulum swings in at least two directions in order to move, you may still have to determine from there which one you need to explore.

Your simplest tool may be a small stick with the end sharpened into a point (though not *too* sharp!). Go to a place where you suspect there may be a power spot, and ask your totems to point the stick in the direction you should go. After making sure you're sheltered enough from the wind that it won't affect your results, toss the stick up in the air but not directly above you, as you don't want the pointy end to hit you. Wherever the pointy end is facing when it lands, that's the way you should go. Don't feel as though you have to go hacking your way through the bushes; find the nearest path or trail going in that general direction and use that until you think you're getting close. Once you get to the place, you can determine whether it's a potential power spot for you.

Depending on where you live, you may find that your power spots overlap with the sacred places of indigenous cultures extant and not. You may choose to not use these places out of respect if the indigenous people prefer not to share and especially if the place was taken from them violently. On the other hand, almost every place has hosted some significant event for someone somewhere at some point in history, so it's hard to avoid stepping onto someone's memories. My advice is to be respectful and make your decisions with prudence, but don't completely hobble yourself out of fear of offending someone. Where I live in the Northwest, much of the land was taken from the indigenous tribes, most of whom still live here albeit in smaller areas. I act with awareness of that fact, and I also create my own relationships to the land in part to treat it better than my own nonindigenous ancestors did.

Remember not to treat a power spot like your own personal battery. You need to take care of it too. An easy way to do this is to pick up trash left by other people; all but the most remote backcountry areas these days are blighted by our litter. You're also welcome to leave a small offering; I recommend things that are biodegradable and preferably won't be eaten by wildlife. I like leaving a few strands of hair tied to a tree branch; it's a piece of myself, and at most a bird may grab it for nesting material. (Offerings are further discussed in chapter 6.)

What do you actually do with a power spot? Here are a few suggestions:

- As with other places you've done spiritual work, spend time getting to know the place if you haven't already. You might find surprising answers to why a place has such power. It may have been sacred to another culture, or the site of an important historical event. Or it may be home to rare species found nowhere else. In either of these cases it is especially important that you act in ways that preserve the land, to include working with it remotely, which brings me to the next suggestion...

- Find a small item from this place that you can take with you as a physical link to it. If you are unable to take something from it, then find a small item you have at home that you can leave at this place for at least one complete moon cycle, from new moon to new moon. Make sure it's something inert that won't harm the environment there and which won't be damaged by the elements, either; a coin, a natural stone, even a piece of decorative glass (unpainted) will work. Put the item in a place where it's unlikely to be disturbed by other people or animals, or washed away by water. If you bury it in the ground or a hollow in a tree, make sure you're not unnecessarily damaging any plants or fungi or disturbing animals' homes. At the end of the moon cycle, retrieve it, and leave it there again for one moon cycle each year to recharge. You may wish to have two such items so you're never without a physical link to the place.

- See if there's a particular totem associated with the power spot. Great Horsetail, the totem of a primitive plant native to the Northwest, watches over the power spot near my adopted beach, and horsetails grow near the center of the spot. Get to know this totem as you have the others, to include its place in the ecosystem, other totems it interacts with regularly, etc. This totem also is likely to have requests for caring for this place, and may additionally ask you to do some ritual work there on its behalf. This may be something as simple as energetic cleansing (sort of like routine maintenance to go with your litter pickup) or may be a more elaborate celebratory ritual (more on those later in the chapter).

- Of course you can go to this place to recharge like when you're recovering from illness (though make sure your travels and time there aren't making the illness worse— use your physical link if need be) or when you're going through a tough time full of stress. You can also "charge up" in preparation for a big ritual or other spiritual working. You can even bring some energy to someone else if they really need it and you believe they'd respect it for what it is. However, the strongest quality of this place is the simple restorative properties of nature, which have been proven to have measurable positive effects on blood pressure, stress level, and overall health.

- If the place and its totem seems amenable to it, you can bring other people here, too. Be selective; it's not a place to have a big drinking party and huge bonfire (though some power spots seem to enjoy happy celebrations with lots of people more than others). Think more along the lines of introducing particular friends and loved ones who would appreciate the place and perhaps even help you tend it, or having a small group ritual with similarly respectful people. Make sure the physical land can handle the impact of that many people and that you explain to everyone how to walk gently on the land. If you know someone who may benefit from the power spot in the same way you have, you can bring them to it and let them recharge, though it's best to ask permission of the place and its totem first.

- When doing rituals of any sort, you can call on the power spot to add some energy to what you're doing, whether you're physically present in the spot or not. When calling the directions, some people will also call on sacred places in those directions; I myself learned the practice from James Endredy, author of one of my favorite books, *Ecoshamanism: Sacred Practices of Unity, Power, and Earth Healing.*

You may find several power spots to work with as time goes on, so pay attention to where they are in your bioregion:

is there any pattern to their locations?[18] Do they tend to be in particular types of habitat? Are they mainly in wilderness places, or have you also found some urban power spots as well? If they each have a representative totem, are there any relationships among them? What sorts of personalities do they have? Are some friendlier to visitors than others? Do some demand more of you in terms of care and upkeep? Do some only offer you energy selectively, while others freely give as much as you need any time?

If you wish to create a physical link to each power spot you work with, you can keep them in a particular place in your home. You might have an altar of curiosities housing all of them, arranged in a sort of map layout to show where they are in relation to where you live.

Keep in mind that not every place you work with is a power spot. The thing that differentiates a power spot from other locations is its particularly strong energy/personality as well as its ability to recharge and help you in ways other places don't. It doesn't make other places lower in quality or importance; it's a different sort of sacredness.

———

Bishop is well-versed in spiritual practices; he grew up near Albuquerque, New Mexico, in a family that was

---

18. Please don't read too much into this question. In other words, don't plug all the locations into a map and then try really hard to make a picture out of them. It's less about "does this look like a secret symbol on the map?" and more about "are there any characteristics that these places share?"

open to spiritual exploration, though with a healthy dose of skepticism to keep things from going overboard. He was quite young when he first heard about the concept of power spots, and it was something that caught his imagination from the beginning. While he was aware of all the places in and around the city where the tourists were taken to get their "spiritual vibes," none of these seemed so special to him, perhaps because he was so used to them. It wasn't until he was old enough to start hiking and camping by himself that he began to notice places that called out to him. One evening, as he is preparing his camp sheltered by the side of a rocky ridge, he feels compelled to hike up to the top of the ridge. Armed with flashlight and walking staff, he goes up a narrow trail through the brush. Just as he reaches the top of the ridge, he comes out of the shadows and into the moonlight that paints the land silver. He feels a profound connection to this place that he's never felt anywhere else. Suddenly, he's startled by a sound that he thinks may be the snort of a javelina, an animal that hasn't been seen in this area for decades, but after remaining still for several minutes he determines he is alone. Still, the combination of his deep feeling for this place and the seeming echo of a long-gone animal captures his imagination, and upon his return home the next day he decides to look more closely into the personal spiritual implications of this experience.

Bioregional Totems on the Move

While most of the material here is centered on your bioregion and the totems within it, it's also possible to apply much of it to other bioregions as well. Maybe you're traveling and want to greet the place you're going to more properly, or perhaps you need a bit of spiritual help away from your usual power spots and other sacred places. You may have moved away from home to go to school and want to avoid feeling homesick while also making new connections. Maybe that move is permanent and you want to see who your new nonhuman neighbors are.

I already covered this topic some in my previous totem books as they relate to those types of totems (animal and plant or fungus) specifically so if you have one or both of them, you can supplement this section with that information as they complement the material here quite nicely. Even if this book is all you have, the goal is connecting with the totems of a place you wouldn't normally be in and asking them to help you be more at ease with the land (and vice versa).

One way to proceed is to introduce yourself to the totems of a place before you even go there as part of your trip/moving preparation. There are a couple of ways you can do this:

- If the place where you are now and the place you're going have an animal, plant, or fungus in common, you can ask its totem to help you bridge the gap. The same goes for being a part of the same major geological formation, or having waterways that are connected (such as a river and one of its smaller tributaries). It's easier if you have a history with that totem, but you can make this your first contact with them too. In my experience, many totems appreciate the polite gesture you're making and seem willing to help.

- You can also put forth a general call to the totems of the area you're going to for help in being a good guest/new community member in their home. You might ask your current totems for help with this too. If one or more totems from the new place respond, thank them for their presence and go from there.

I like doing a brief ritual to get in touch with these totems. With the help of my own bioregional totems, I focus on the place I'm going to be heading soon, and I think of everything I know about it (having done some pre-ritual research). Then I think or say a small prayer to the totems of the new place, something like the following:

Greetings, Totems and Spirits of [Bioregion/City/etc.]! I am [name], of [bioregional address].[19] I intend to travel to your home soon, and I ask for safe passage and your help in being good to this place. Will one of you guide me in being a good visitor [or community member if you're moving there]? Will you tell me what I must do to treat you and your land well?

---

19. For example, "Lupa, of the Portland Basin where the Willamette meets the Columbia in the shadow of Mt. Hood."

Give them a little time to respond. You may feel a sensation in your gut or the back of your head, similar to whatever you feel when one of your totems contacts you. You may hear a voice in your mind, more like a thought than a physical voice. Or you may have a brief vision in your head of a totem responding. That may be all the affirmation you get, or they may talk with you more once you've noticed them. If they request a gift or offering after you've arrived, do your best to comply. Usually it's going to be something simple like a bit of your time spent with them outside, or a small donation to a local organization that helps the land and its inhabitants. Totems may also make a few requests of you, such as avoiding particular power spots they prefer to only use with those who live there.

While you're in the new place even for a short period of time, do your best to familiarize yourself with its inhabitants and other natural features instead of focusing on your trip itinerary. When I go to a new place, I try to get at least one good hike in or a little time in a park. I also pay attention to the wildlife (to include in urban areas), and the contours of the land, even if it's paved over. It shows the place that you're interested in it and respect it in the same way you respect your home, and it's a neat way to add more value to your trip. And if it's a stressful trip rather than a vacation, the focus on the entire community helps me feel better and gives me strength to face the challenges.

If you're moving to the place, you can start using the rest of the exercises in this book to create new totemic connections over time. If you're only visiting and need a bit of spiritual help, recall the concept of tertiary totems from chapter 4: this is the sort of totemic relationship you'll be invoking here.

Just as you did a ritual asking to be a part of their community for a short while, you can do a similar call for the totems' help.

———

Laura is on vacation with her wife, Josie, at a resort. While they're driving down the highway, their rental car blows a tire, and they manage to make it safely to the shoulder. Upon pulling out the spare to change it, they find it's flat as well, so they call the rental company for assistance. The day is hot and they don't have a lot of water; Josie's not feeling well in the heat and is quite cranky. The whole situation makes Laura feel very stressed out, so she takes a few moments to walk in the field next to the road. She silently calls out to the totems of the land, asking for their help in calming down a bit. A cool breeze suddenly picks up around her and she smells the flowers of an American wisteria nearby; she was so busy being frustrated that she walked right by it. In her heart, she feels its totem wishing her a little peace, even if she isn't one of the pollinators the scent was originally meant for. Laura breathes in the lovely aroma a bit more, then goes back to the car to keep Josie company until help arrives. Before they leave, she makes a donation to a local botanical garden that keeps some American wisteria vines, among other things.

Before you go back home, it's a good practice to thank the totems for allowing you to share their home with you for a little while. You can do a similar ritual to the greeting one, and leave another offering if it seems appropriate. If you think you'll be visiting again sometime, make sure and let them know and ask for safe passage in the future.

Can you still keep in touch with the totems of an older place even when you've moved somewhere new? Of course! Just like friendships made in your previous home, you can still keep in touch with the totems. If you're willing and able, you can go back and visit them periodically. If that's not possible for you, that's okay—you can still maintain those relationships and the good that has come from them. Some people might find great relief in leaving a place for good, but the spiritual experiences they had in past challenging times strengthened them forever. It's a very good idea to keep a memory of whomever helped them, totems included.

Practices of Action

One of the great things the human species has evolved is self-awareness. While it can sometimes be a burden, it's also an opportunity to consciously improve ourselves as people, a community, and a species. One of the benefits of totemism is having access to a variety of spiritual beings who are experts in their own species and who also have plenty of experience with humans, too, making it easier to learn new lessons we might not get in the human world.

Self-Evolution

No one in the world does not face challenges and have something they'd like to make better about themselves. Self-evolution isn't about being a broken person who needs fixing but instead taking strengths, whatever they may be, and using them as a framework to change the parts of the self we'd like to be different. Sometimes this means working within restrictions you can't do anything about such as chronic physical or mental illness, and some lessons are about adapting to these parameters to the best of your ability. There is no competition with other people here; your goal shouldn't be to become better than someone else, especially if the other person (or people) don't work with the same set of restrictions you do. Others might face challenges you don't, and as much as it may be a cliché I firmly believe it's good practice not to compare your behind-the-scenes to someone else's highlight reel, as it were.

What sorts of things could you change with the help of totems? Just about anything within your natural ability to change, really. The totems aren't doing the work *for* you; they instead offer guidance and support throughout the process, providing you with more tools to get the job done.

The first thing you want to do is to decide what you want to change in yourself. It's okay to start small; keep your goals realistic. Nothing is more detrimental to your confidence than setting too big a goal for yourself, being unable to meet it, and feeling like a failure as a result. Even small changes add up, so don't be afraid to try some baby steps before moving on to bigger things. Here are some possible starting points:

- What's a bad habit you'd like to change? Is there a good habit you don't currently have but you'd like to develop? Perhaps you want to exercise more regularly, or stop apologizing unnecessarily, for example.

- How about new skills and other areas of interest? Maybe you want to start researching a particular culture's history or learn how to play a new musical instrument.

- You may have health challenges that make life a little tougher and want to find solutions in addition to what you're already trying. Perhaps depression makes it harder for you to get through your day much of the time and you'd like to explore ways to make things a little easier. Or you may have a health problem that restricts your diet and you're having a difficult time adjusting.

You may be wondering how totems can help you figure out how a violin works or remind you to get to the gym. While these activities are unique to humans, there are qualities of totems that can help you achieve these goals.

Let's say the violin is your new challenge, but every time in the past you've tried to learn to play a new instrument, you've gotten frustrated because you don't think you're good enough, and instead of continuing to practice to get better, you quit and feel bad about yourself. You might then ask a local totem for help with being more persistent, and perhaps less self-conscious. If you're in certain parts of Africa or Asia, the totem Honey Badger might answer your request. Popular tongue-in-cheek nature videos aside, honey badgers are quite persistent creatures and there's not a whole lot in this world that bothers them.[20] The next time you try picking up that violin again and start to get frustrated because it doesn't sound perfect, Honey Badger may remind you to keep trying anyway and not care who's listening because all they're hearing is someone in the process of becoming more awesome.

Above all, remember that totemic work is never meant to be a substitute for professional medical care, physical or mental. That said, it can complement professional help nicely in many cases.

As a case in point, I've had Generalized Anxiety Disorder for much of my life. While I've never had to take medications for it, I have been in therapy for several years, and it has helped. I've also done a lot of totemic work to help my ability to handle this condition better on a daily basis. Red Fox is one of my totems; along with helping me connect with a couple of different bioregions, Red Fox has also helped me to calm some of the sharper manifestations of my anxiety, particularly those related to fear-borne anger and other reactions. This totem has shown me how to be less reactionary and temper my responses to common anxiety triggers so I am not wasting my energy or overreacting to things that aren't actually threats. While foxes are quite energetic creatures, they don't waste energy running from any possible threat; they take in as much information

---

20. Specifically the video at https://www.youtube.com/ watch?v=4r7wHMg5Yjg. Please be aware that while it's pretty informative, it also contains strong language. However, if you do ever work with Honey Badger as a totem, the video can be rather inspirational, and from my experience the totem finds it pretty entertaining.

as they can before deciding whether to run or not; like other predators, they also learn to show similar prudence when deciding whether to chase a particular prey animal. The wisdom regarding fight or flight, chase or wait, has been a good model to emulate with my anxiety, and while other totems could potentially have taught me this as well, Red Fox happened to be the one to get the lesson through to me effectively.

There will always be some things totems can't help with; they can't magically change the chemistry in my or anyone's brain to make us "normal." They can't make an ex-partner love you again, nor can they bring you lots of money. What they can do is help you be more effective at finding solutions for the problems you face both through advice on how to proceed and offering more tools for you to use.

Using Your Bioregional Map

Remember back in chapter 2 when I had you make a map of your bioregion? It's time to pull it out again!

If you haven't been using it to keep track of the totems you've been working with and places that you've explored, you may wish to update it. This can be a very worthwhile exercise in and of itself, as it gives you a better visual of how much you're learned and the connections you've made. Depending on how large your map is, you can also use it as a base for an altar of curiosities holding the physical representations of your power spots; if you don't have much horizontal space but you do have a nice, big wall the map hangs on, tie strings around the objects and hang them from the map with a tack stuck into the place each object came from. (Another possible option is using stick-on Velcro, though it may damage some fragile items like feathers or the bark on a dried stick.)

Like these sacred items, the bioregional map can also be a stand-in for a power spot if you aren't able to get to the place itself. Let's say one of your power spots is threatened by development, and you want to send some protective energy to the place in addition to contacting your elected officials and other pertinent parties to help preserve it. You might fill a small pouch with items associated with protection and place your personal energy into it. Tack or otherwise attach it to the corresponding place on the map with a prayer to send the energy to your power spot.

If the place in question isn't a power spot, the same concept still applies, especially if you aren't able to physically get to the location itself. If you're doing a ritual to augment activism to protect a place or the beings living there, bring the map into your ritual space if it isn't there already. Call on any totems associated with the location in question, and ask them to add their energy to the efforts you're making. You might focus some of this energy into letters to be sent to the appropriate officials elected or otherwise or bring it into yourself to give you strength in hands-on efforts like removing invasive species or educating other people about the threats to this place. Don't forget to take this opportunity to ask the totems for their suggestions on how else you may be able to help. You can leave the letters tacked to the map overnight and mail them the next day or write a statement of your intent to help this place and attach it to its location on the map.

The map itself makes a good general meditative focus. Once you have it up-to-date with records of your totemic work, spend some time studying it. Let the marks and notes remind you of your progress. The map might also remind you of a totem or place you haven't checked in a while, or you may feel inspired to explore somewhere new. You can even engage in a little "dartboard divination" if you aren't sure where to go next. Ask your totems for a little guidance as you take a dart, close your eyes, and throw it at the map (make sure there's nothing near the map you don't want to accidentally get stuck in case you miss entirely!). If you're working with a digital version, expand the map to fill your screen, close your eyes and then randomly move the mouse around until you feel compelled to stop. Wherever the cursor is, let that be the next place you go (unless you missed the map entirely, in which case try again).

A Rite for Invasive Species

Not every species in your bioregion may be native to that place. With the dawn of agriculture, we started to get very good at transporting plants, animals, and fungi from one place to another—too good, really. We moved species all over the world without thinking of potential consequences, and today there are very few locations that don't have at least a couple of new additions care of *Homo sapiens*. (I'll leave the argument of whether we're invasive or not for another time.)

A species being invasive doesn't necessarily mean it is bad; not all invaders are inherently toxic. While fields of domesticated wheat, originating from the Near East, are abundant worldwide, without deliberate human cultivation they eventually end up supplanted by native plants. However, many invasive species cause serious disruption to the ecosystem they're introduced to, even once we've stopped helping them. The domestic cat originated in Africa (quite possibly Egypt in specific), but it has accompanied us around the world; pet and feral alike, outdoor cats have caused the extinction of several species of native small mammal, bird, and reptile, and they have contributed to the endangerment of many others.[21]

And the invasives aren't just domesticated, either. From nutria to cane toads, kudzu to Himalayan blackberry, invasive species are wreaking havoc on native ecosystems worldwide, threatening the carefully balanced systems of interrelationships that have coevolved over thousands of years. They crowd out species that serve as food, shelter, and pollination for other species and compete for the resources that remain. Invasive predators may decimate prey species and out-compete native predators. The litany of destruction goes on.

While there are a few cases where it's a bad idea to remove the invasive species—certain plants in Hawaii that used to be pollinated by now-extinct native birds are now pollinated by the invasives that out-competed them—for the most part the common policy is to eradicate invasives. These species have

---

21. For those who want the numbers, a recent study shows that cats in the U.S. alone kill 12.3 *billion* (not million) wild mammals a year, along with 2.4 billion birds, most of which are native species rather than introduced ones. See Angier in the Bibliography for more information. If you have cats, you may wish to either keep them indoors, or supervise them when they're outside, both for their safety and that of the creatures around them.

totems, too, which can cause quite the quandary for a dedicated totemist. After all, many totems just want to see their physical counterparts thrive, and some are supportive of invasion (much to the chagrin of their native counterparts). Killing a living being is never a beautiful thing, and it deprives that animal, plant, fungus, etc. of its chance to interact with this world…no small act, if you think about it.

If a threatened ecosystem is to survive, the species that co-evolved need a chance to regain their balance without outside competition. I have put in plenty of volunteer time pulling up English ivy, Himalayan blackberry, and other invasives in Oregon, and I like to do a ritual of apology to their totems before I start.

Go to your ritual space, wherever that may be; take a small piece of the species to be removed (if possible) or a representative of it, even a picture printed out from the Internet. After taking a few moments to prepare yourself, hold the item in your hands gently but firmly, and call upon its totem to join you if it will. Once it arrives, say the following:

Dear [Totem], in my hands I hold your child. In my hands I hold one who is watched over by you and dear to you. Soon these same hands will destroy more like this one, those who breathe the same air I do and drink the same water and live on the same land. It is not my wish to anger you, and if I could leave them be, I would. But they are in the wrong place due to my own kind; if this place is to survive, your children must go, remaining only in the places where they belong.

> *I ask for your forgiveness as I kill and destroy. I ask that you not hold this against me but instead understand that I only do what I feel is right. Many of your children die every day; many more are born. I ask that I be given the same consideration as the other beings that prey upon your children: I do not wish you and yours harm, I only act out of necessity.*
>
> *I offer you a place in my home if you will take it. I ask you, too, if there are things I can do to help your children in the places where they do belong. I wish only to make amends for what I am about to do.*

Wait for a few moments to see if the totem responds and have whatever conversation may ensue. Once you are done communing with the totem, place the representation in a special spot in your home; it may be an existing altar of curiosities or one dedicated especially to invasive species. The totem may or may not choose to work with you further, but it's a good gesture to make nonetheless.

If you are legally hunting or trapping invasive animal species, you may wish to read Miles Olson's excellent book, *The Compassionate Hunter's Guidebook: Hunting From the Heart*. Far from being a yee-haw guide to getting the buck with the biggest rack, it reteaches modern hunters how to respect the animals they are hunting, and to view the hunt as a sacred act. Olson is also quite thorough in demonstrating how to truly use every part of the animal (with deer as the example), down to making broth from the bones, soup from the head, and a gelatin dessert from the skin.

I also discuss the respectful use of animal, plant, and fungus remains in my writing. *Plant and Fungus Totems* contains a chapter on working with what I call leaves and caps, and other parts of the book emphasize care in handling these sacred remains. All of my books on animal totems and related practices include some information on working with hides and bones and the like, though *Skin Spirits: The Spiritual and Magical Use of Animal Parts* is entirely dedicated to the topic for those who are especially interested.

Does it help if the remains of the invasive species being destroyed are put to good use? Absolutely. As one good model of this concept, there's a local nonprofit organization where I live called Rewild Portland (http://www.rewildportland.com/), that teaches people "primitive" skills like wool felting, animal tracking, wildcrafting, and the like. Part of their curriculum involves harvesting invasive species of animal and plant; you can learn how to trap and cook nutria and how to weave a basket or hat out of English ivy. Even if you can't do something quite that elaborate, at least try to compost what you kill, being careful not to spread plant seeds or fungus spores. In case it needs to be emphasized, the deaths of invasive animals should be as quick and painless as possible; if you are not eating them yourself, leave their carcasses where scavengers can safely consume them.

If you can't bring yourself to destroy invasive species, you can help by supporting those who raise and release or plant native species. You can also choose to not introduce more invasive species in your garden and yard and gently educate others about the negative effects of these introduced beings.

Practices of Celebration

We human critters like to mark special occasions and dates with sacred practices. Bioregional totemism offers ample opportunities for celebration as the seasons change and the land shifts and flows with them. Not all of these may be joyful occasions; the Rite of Farewell can be a somber experience, especially if this is the first time a totem has opted to leave your life. You may wish to create observances for particular times or events that are especially important to you and the land you live with; let these following pages be inspiration.

Totemic Anniversaries

Totems don't have birthdays, as much fun as their parties could be! The closest you might get to a date of birth is the birth of the first member of a species to develop a trait that will one day help its descendants evolve into another species, but evolution is such a gradual process that it's useless to pinpoint when a new species is born.

Instead of pinpointing that moment of evolution in time, you can observe the anniversary of when you and a totem first found each other, the first ritual you did together, or any other important event you shared. Some totems may also ask you to observe a particular day in the year significant to them whether for celebration or more somber purposes. A totem's special day could include the point of the year when their physical counterparts begin their migration to summer territories, when the last danger of frost has passed by, or the anniversary of an important habitat being destroyed.

There's no single proper way to enact any of these rites. Here are some potential options:

- Write a poem or other piece describing the reason this day is special and read it to the totem. If you absolutely believe you can't write well enough for this, look for a myth, story, piece of nature writing, or another artifact that talks about the totem you wish to honor today. You could also work with other art forms like visual arts, music, etc.

- Go to a power spot or other location the totem is fond of and spend some time there together. If the area needs tending such as litter pickup or invasive species removal, you have a great opportunity to make an offering of your effort. You can also make an offering while you're there; some suggestions appear in chapter 6. Even if you can't take a field trip to a particular location, you can still visit the totem wherever you are through guided meditation.

- Engage in a bit of shapeshifting dance, embodying the concept that imitation really is the sincerest form of flattery. With whatever drumming or other music you prefer in the background (silence is fine too), begin to move like the totem or the forces that created it. It might be the slow, ponderous grinding of tectonic plates and the occasional burst of lava, or the flitting, high-octane acrobatics of hummingbirds. Don't worry about getting it just right;

this isn't about being a professional dancer, and you don't have to dance in front of others if you don't want to. Even if you're confined to a chair or bed, move as much as you're able or dance in your imagination. As you dance, invite the totem to join you in your celebration, and perhaps help you to become a little more like them in the process.

Rites of Cycles and Changes

It seems that almost every single book on nature spirituality these days has some section on how to celebrate the solstices, equinoxes, and the points midway between them. There's good reason for this; our ancestors and many indigenous people today are much more aware of the seasonal cycles than the rest of us. We've lost that attention to natural details like where on the horizon the sun and moon rise and set at a given time in the year or when migratory birds reappear. By marking certain special times throughout the seasons, we begin to regain our awareness and remember why it's important to not be so tunnel-visioned on ourselves and our species. There are natural processes much greater than us that would still go on whether we were around or not, and it's humbling in a good way to be reminded of this.

The equinoxes, as you may know, are the two times throughout the year where day and night are of equal length. One marks the start of spring; the other kicks off autumn. The summer solstice is when the sun is the furthest north, and the winter solstice is when it's gone as south as it will go for the year in the northern hemisphere; the two solstices are reversed in the southern hemisphere. Because the equinoxes and solstices mark certain notable points in the travel of the sun, they make good checkpoints throughout the year. They're also far enough apart that plenty of changes occur in the natural world, and we can use these occasions to see what's developed as the seasons turn.

Some people also like to mark the cross-quarters, the points between the solstices and equinoxes. The year is divided up into roughly eight six-week chunks with a few extra days each, again long enough for changes to happen in nature but not so far apart that we miss important events.

The lunar cycle is another option for a celebratory calendar. Each lunar cycle is twenty-nine days long from new moon to new moon or full moon to full moon. Many people like to use the full moon as a time to celebrate because the silver shining light in the sky is a good reminder that it's time to check in with the world again, and some believe the full moon phase is especially sacred in and of itself. If you like being active outdoors at night, there's nothing quite like the full moon making things almost as bright as day to accentuate the experience.

I've only given you suggestions; you're welcome to celebrate whenever you like, whether that's daily, weekly, or whenever it rains. But always ask yourself: "what am I celebrating?" It could be the totems themselves, as mentioned above, or you can also celebrate the intricate world you and they share, the movement of the stars, and the rising and falling of the tides. You might believe the day you harvest the first vegetables from your garden or find the first edible mushrooms of the year is a special occasion—and these don't have to fall on the same day every year. In fact, if you like to throw a little picnic and barbecue whenever the salmon begin to run in a nearby river each year, you can keep track of whether they're early, late, or right on time this year. Think of a celebration as another way to be mindful of your bioregion, its cycles and residents, and the totems watching over them all.

I'm not going to fill a bunch of pages with a ritual for every solstice, equinox, cross-quarter, and full moon you're required to enact every year, word for word. Instead I'll leave it up to you when you want to celebrate and how. You can take some ideas from the previous section, or you can look at the following ritual and ones in other books on Neopagan and other animistic nature celebrations as inspiration for creating your own sacred rites.

The Journey to the Sun is a ritual I originally created for Sunfest, a summer solstice celebration held every year by Other Worlds of Wonder (http://www.owow.org), a nonprofit organization here in Oregon working toward purchasing land for spiritual purposes. It leads participants through a walking pathworking; at regular intervals along the path, different types of totems —animals, plants, etc.—speak with the participants embodied through the ritual facilitators. They all explain how they depend on the sun in different ways, from photosynthesis for plants to the heat that influences the climate. The final stage brings us to the sun itself (also the totem Sun), appropriate for the summer solstice.

While it was created for group use, you can also adapt it as a solitary rite, simply meeting with each totem in turn. Group or solo, ideally you'll perform the ritual in a large field or system of trails where you can walk from one place to the next in between each stage of the rite, but if all you have is a room in your home, just walk once or twice around the perimeter of the room from one stage to the next. If nothing else, perform the ritual in your head, using your imagination to create the perfect sacred space.

One optional part of this ritual involves giving participants a small stone or other memento at each station that carries the energy of the totems met there. You're welcome to include this part of the ritual or not; again, I offer this up not as holy writ but inspiration. Alter it as needed—for example, I don't make as much reference to the totems of individual species as I do elsewhere in this book, and you could choose more specific totems. Or you can swap out totems more appropriate to where you live. I do ask that if you use it with others that you give me a bit of credit.

If you're doing this ritual with a group, you'll need to determine ahead of time who will take which part(s). There are several totems that speak at each station plus a couple of guardians who make sure the other participants stay safe as you move along. The first time I led this ritual, I had to take on the part of every totem evoked in the ritual, and the only other people active in the ritual were four guardians; the rest of the attendees preferred to simply observe and be led through the pathworking. While it was exhausting to embody so many totems in such a short period of time, they were incredibly helpful as I called on each, and the ritual was quite a success.

Throughout the ritual I will be referring to you (or whoever leads the ritual) as the leader. Some of this may not apply if you're on your own; change things as needed.

Journey to the Sun Ritual

Participants all gather at the beginning of the path, forming a semicircle.

Leader: Welcome to the Journey to the Sun. This will be a walking pathworking; we will have approximately forty-five to sixty minutes of walking and standing. If anyone needs any accommodations, please let one of our guardians know.

To help you and those around you to focus on the ritual, we ask that you please observe ritual silence now and throughout the ritual, except when prompted to speak or chant. Also, as we proceed from station to station, we ask that you walk silently in single file. Should you need assistance or to leave the ritual with an escort, please quietly notify one of our guardians.

Let us begin. Close your eyes if you are comfortable, and focus on your breathing. Slow your breath and feel the air as it enters your nose and mouth, flowing down your throat and into your lungs, and then back out. Visualize the oxygen absorbing into the tissues of your lungs, and the carbon dioxide being expelled.

Now focus on your feet. Feel the soles of your feet against the ground. Feel the weight of your body pressing down on them. Imagine your feet sinking down, past your ankles, into the earth below, rooting themselves. Send your awareness down through the dirt, into the bedrock, and think of just how vast the Earth is compared to this tiny patch of dirt you occupy in this moment.

Keep your feet rooted in the ground, and now visualize the top of your head. Feel the freedom of the open space all around your head, and the air surrounding you. Send your awareness expanding from the top of your head all the way up into the openness of the sky above and around you. Think of how much larger the atmosphere is compared to the tiny bit of air you bring in with every breath.

Bring that awareness of the vast sky back down to your body. And draw that rooted darkness of the ground up into your body. And let these things meet within you, where the Sky kisses the Earth, right here in this liminal space between Earth and Sky. And as we walk this path, know that as long as you have the Earth below you and the Sky above you, no harm will come to you.

I ask that you now follow me and the guardians, single file, in silence, and enter our path.

Proceed to first station, leader in front, one guardian at the rear, and any other guardians dispersed throughout the line.

First station: Carnivore totems are here.

Wolf: I am Wolf. I am the apex predator; I and my pack run across plains and forests. The Sun shines down upon us as we hunt our prey, as we tear to pieces tender flesh that once lived and breathed and kicked. The meat we rend with our teeth and consume becomes our own flesh and blood and bone.

Serpent: I am Serpent. I engulf my prey; I swallow it whole. Deep down into my belly I take my prey, and it slowly becomes a part of me. I am made of the mouse and the rat, the worm and the insect. I bask in the Sun as my prey digests within me.

Swallow: I am Swallow. I swoop and fly and arc through the air with the Sun on my wings. Though I am small, I am a formidable hunter; I can catch hundreds of insects in an afternoon, and their delicate bodies become food for me and my young.

Wolf: And you, too, human animals, come from a long line of meat-eaters, even if you yourself do not eat meat.

Serpent: The animals you eat become a part of you in body and spirit. Life and death are transformations, changing one thing into another.

Swallow: Deer becomes wolf, mouse becomes serpent, fly becomes swallow. Take our gift to you before you go. And as you continue on your journey, remember these words and speak them as you go:

All three: Flesh into flesh, blood into blood. Flesh into flesh, blood into blood. Flesh into flesh, blood into blood.

Leader and guardians pick up the chant and encourage all participants to do the same, chanting as they continue single file to the next station. As each leaves the station they take a small stone from the bowl before the Carnivore totems; this will be repeated at every other station. Wolf, Serpent, and Swallow wait until all participants leave, then proceed back to the ninth station where the Sun is; this station should have food and water available, so those embodying the totems can ground and eat and prepare for the participants' return.

Second station: Herbivore totems are here.

Rabbit: I am Rabbit. I am she who runs quickly with long ears sifting through sounds in the weeds. The sunlight dries the dew from my fur in the morning, and I consume the sunlight and soil through the greenery I eat. I nibble at the grass and the gardens and hope that my feet may be swift enough to save me from you.

Cow: I am Cow. I am the descendant of wild ancestors, but now I am tame. Within your fields I graze, by your hands I die. I live my life to transform grass and corn into meat and milk for you to consume.

Locust: I am Locust. Alone I am small and vulnerable. But in the thousands we are powerful, consuming all the greenery in sight. I fly from bush to tree to field leaving bare, empty land. No wonder that some of you recapture what was stolen by eating us in turn.

Rabbit: Oh humans, your rise to the top was built on our flesh and blood. It was our meat that let your brains and bodies grow ever larger. Take care that your need to consume us does not turn you into plagues scouring the land.

Cow: As we change the plants into flesh and bone, so do you change the land to meet your needs. You transform inside and out, and we all feel the effects.

Locust: Clover becomes Rabbit, corn becomes Cow, leaf becomes Locust, and all these become wolves and humans. Take our gift to you before you go. And as you continue on your journey, remember these words and speak them as you go:

All three: Body consumed, strength carried on! Body consumed, strength carried on! Body consumed, strength carried on!

Leader and guardians pick up the chant, and encourage all participants to do the same, chanting as they continue single file to the next station. Rabbit, Cow, and Locust wait until all participants leave, then proceed back to the ninth station to ground and eat and prepare for the participants' return.

Third station: Plant totems are here.

Hemlock Tree: I am Hemlock Tree. At the top of the canopy I stretch my branches forth and up; my life is a race to the top to steal as much of the Sun from the others as possible. My roots are a long, tangled network in the soil.

Wheat: I am Wheat. Thousands of years ago I taught you to farm; now I stretch wide across lands my ancestors never knew. I live for one year before I am cut down, my stalks burned or left to rot in the Sun and rain.

Bracken: I am Bracken, of the ancient line of ferns. Deep in the undergrowth I make the most of what Sun trickles down, and I soak in the life-giving rain. Where I am, the forest is healthy and well-watered, even if it is dark and cool.

Hemlock Tree: Your loggers discard me as a junk tree, my wood not suitable for planks. Yet I am so much more than dead wood; I am homes for animals, I am provider of nutrients and nurse logs when I die, and you breathe in the air that I exhale.

Wheat: You grow me alone in a monocultured, fertilizer-soaked fields; sometimes you don't even let the soil rest from year to year. Remember your farming roots, and take the greatest care of the land we all need to live.

Bracken: If my ancestors had not populated the land first, you would not be here today. For millions of years we have transformed the Sun into sugars and the poisons into breathable air. Take our gift to you before you go. And as you continue on your journey, remember these words and speak them as you go:

All three: Sun into food, poisons begone! Sun into food, poisons begone! Sun into food, poisons begone!

Leader and guardians pick up the chant, and encourage all participants to do the same, chanting as they continue single file to the next station. Hemlock Tree, Wheat, and Bracken wait until all participants leave, then proceed back to the ninth station to ground and eat and prepare for the participants' return.

Fourth station: Fungus totems are here.

Portobello Mushroom: I am Portobello, of the mushrooms. From a tiny spore I turn into a magnificent fleshy cap, and I devour the rotted, Sun-soaked cells of fallen plants. Unlike many of my toadstool kin, I will feed you, not poison you.

Baker's Yeast: I am Baker's Yeast. I inhabit the soft folds of dough made from wheat and rice and corn, turning the plant sugars into fuel and producing air that makes the bread rise. Our relationship is a happy accident beneficial to us both; you get your bread, and my descendants are encouraged to live and grow well.

Soil Mycelium: I am Soil Mycelium. Out of the reach of the Sun's rays, I break down the remains of all those who have died, and I transform them into small, edible packets. I run through the soil I have created, wrapping around the roots of plants and helping them sift the nutrients from the rest. I am the digestive system in the dirt.

Portobello Mushroom: We fungi take death and transform it into life. We eat what no others will or can consume.

Baker's Yeast: We have even learned to consume the things you create, from processed bread dough to the oil you spill on land and in water.

Soil Mycelium: You may not know most of us exist, and yet without us life could not be as it is. Take our gift to you before you go. And as you continue on your journey, remember these words, and speak them as you go:

All three: Sun into soil, death into life! Sun into soil, death into life! Sun into soil, death into life!

Leader and guardians pick up the chant, and encourage all participants to do the same, chanting as they continue single file to the next station. Portobello Mushroom, Baker's Yeast, and Soil Mycelium wait until all participants leave, then proceed back to the ninth station to ground and eat and prepare for the participants' return.

Fifth station: Soil totems are here.

Forest Loam: I am the rich Loam of the rain forests; the Sun only dances with me on occasion. The rains bring nutrients and much-needed hydration, and I soak in every drop I can. I am made from the deep red rotting cores of trees and the tiny bones of birds.

Farming Field: I am a Farming Field; I was once grassland and forest, now cleared and put to human use. Where once I grew many plants under the Sun, now I only grow a few or one alone. Many times I struggle to replace the nutrients taken too quickly from me while my mycelia burn and die from chemical fertilizers.

Desert Dust: I am the Desert Dust. I am stingy with my favors, for I receive few from the sky; here in the rain shadow of the mountains, the Sun-soaked air steals the moisture before I get it. My plants and animals trade nutrients carefully and carve out an existence using whatever they can.

Forest Loam: I am only so rich because so many nutrients are traded here. The more of my trees you take and don't replace, the poorer I become.

Farming Field: I am the result of too much taken and not enough given back…or replaced with toxins. Without balance, the Sun may dry me out too much.

Desert Dust: I am the driest of all, and yet I am resilient. Someday I may be lush and full again, but for now I am a reminder that even here the soil supports life, Sun into plants, and plants into animals. Take our gift to you before you go. And as you continue on your journey, remember these words, and speak them as you go:

All three: Sun into soil, roots into Earth! Sun into soil, roots into Earth!

Leader and guardians pick up the chant, and encourage all participants to do the same, chanting as they continue single file to the next station. Forest Loam, Farming Field, and Desert Dust wait until all participants leave, then proceed back to the ninth station to ground and eat and prepare for the participants' return.

Sixth station: Atmospheric totems are here.

Wind: I am Wind. The Sun warms my back as I flow over the land, sometimes speeding me up and sometimes slowing me down. I change the weather from place to place as I travel.

Precipitation: I am Precipitation. The Wind carries me along; sometimes I am rain, sometimes I am fog or dew, and sometimes I become snow and ice. Sometimes there is so little of me I never touch the ground at all.

Wind: Without the Sun-fueled atmosphere overhead, the land would have no character; the soil would be dry and dead. Without the interplay of air and water in the sky, the animals and plants would live only in the sea, if at all.

Precipitation: The Sun and the land and the Wind cause me to fall unevenly, but I am the bringer of life wherever I am. If they were not moving me around, pulling me up from the waters and back into the air, life on Earth would grind to a halt.

Wind: Take our gift to you before you go. And as you continue on your journey, remember these words, and speak them as you go:

Both: Sun moves the Wind, Water, and Life! Sun moves the Wind, Water, and Life!

Leader and guardians pick up the chant, and encourage all participants to do the same, chanting as they continue single file to the next station. Wind and Precipitation wait until all participants leave, then proceed back to the ninth station to ground and eat and prepare for the participants' return.

Seventh station: The totem Ocean is here.

Ocean: I am the Ocean, the great body of water that has covered most of the earth's surface for billions of years. While each part of me is distinct in its shape and inhabitants, I serve to change the weather and even the climate wherever I am. As the Sun warms me or draws away throughout the year, so the atmosphere above me shifts and flows. I build weather systems in my centers, and then I toss them upon the land to let them run. Without me, the earth would be lifeless. Take my gift to you before you go. And as you continue on your journey, remember these words, and speak them as you go:

Ocean: Waves of change, ocean to sky! Waves of change, ocean to sky!

Leader and guardians pick up the chant, and encourage all participants to do the same, chanting as they continue single file to the next station. Ocean waits until all participants leave, then proceeds back to the ninth station to ground and eat and prepare for the participants' return.

Eighth station: The totems of animals of the deep ocean are here.

Anglerfish: I am Anglerfish. I am one of the creatures who dwell far past where the Sun's rays can go; I am one of the nightmare beings with sharp teeth and glowing skin. I am unlike anything else you have ever seen.

Giant Isopod: I am Giant Isopod. I crawl along the bottom of the ocean, scavenging what I can. Without the power of the Sun to create food here, I move slowly, I evolve slowly, and the centuries seem to flow so slowly in my deep ocean bed.

Thermophile: I am a Thermophile of the Deep Sea Vents. Instead of the heat of the Sun, I live far down in the ocean where the very crust of the earth is cracked and the water flows so hot no one else can live here.

Anglerfish: While I have long shed my need for the Sun, my ancestors far above me grew from tiny one-celled animals into complex beings, powered by sunlight through their food. We moved down here over time but would never have come to be otherwise.

Giant Isopod: The Sun-loving animals and plants that die and drift down here are part of how I thrive. There is little for me to hunt and scavenge here in the depths, and each carcass that comes from above is a gift from the Sun.

Thermophile: Even here, the vents I need to live wouldn't exist without the Sun, for the earth would cool too much and its plates would seal up forever. Take our gift to you before you go. And as you continue on your journey, remember these words, and speak them as you go:

All three: Far below Sun, we still survive! Far below Sun, we still survive!

Leader and guardians pick up the chant and encourage all participants to do the same, chanting as they continue single file to the next station. Anglerfish, Giant Isopod, and Thermophile wait until all participants leave, then proceed to the ninth station. Because they immediately precede the ninth station, those who play these parts in the ritual should have enough endurance to do their work in the ninth station right after their work in the eighth.

Ninth station: Sun totem.

Participants all file silently into the station and make a big circle. In the center is the Sun hidden behind a curtain, along with the various beings from previous stations out in the open.

Leader: We have walked through many lands now, of animals and plants and soil and water and so many other things that rely on the Sun. But now we need to call the Sun forth, for without it none of us would be here. I ask now that the beings we have met come forth and remind us of their chants. We will chant these all together to ask the Sun to join us!

At this point, the totems divide the participants into eight groups, one for each of the chants that were learned, while the guard-

ians place themselves at regular intervals around the circle to keep watch over the participants. Each group is reminded of its chant. Then the leader goes around, starting with the first station's group, and has them start chanting the first chant of the animals, then moves to the next and reminds them of the chant of the plants, "lighting up" each group until all eight groups are chanting in unison, each group with a different chant learned along the way.

Chanting continues; leader directs everyone to gradually speed up the chant using a drum. If the groups get off-rhythm with each other, that's okay. At the height of the chanting, the leader calls forth the Sun as loudly as she can.

Leader: Great Sun above us, I ask you to join us *now!*

The Sun comes out from behind the curtain and motions the chanters to be silent.

Sun: I am the Sun. My heat and my light have powered the wind and the waves, the plants and the animals. My rays have warmed the soil and the waters. And they have warmed and fed and sheltered and protected all of you, and all of your ancestors and your fellow beings on this planet. For your chants and your acknowledgement I thank you, and I offer you one final gift to complete this ritual.

The Sun goes around and hands a small token to each of the participants.

Sun: And now it is time for you to enjoy some of the fruits and other foods I have helped to create. Ground yourself in the earth, feel the sunlight (even through the clouds), and reflect on the journey you have made to be here.

All present partake of the food and drink, and people may rest as needed.

The Rite of Farewell

Occasionally a totem will leave you. Whether temporarily or permanently, it may let you know that it's time to part ways, or it may simply disappear from your life. It's also possible that you feel a need to move on and ask the totem to respect your wish. This is not something to take personally, but you may still feel the need for closure; this rite is meant to help with that process. Some people choose to enact this ritual at the end of the relationship. Others wait until a particular time of the year, such as the Winter Solstice, for an energy more conducive to letting go, or the Spring Equinox for new beginnings.

Collect together any representations you have of the totem, like pictures, statues, ritual tools, and so forth. Put them on your altar or other working space. Open the ritual space without a purification first; simply set up the space and call on whatever guardian or helper beings you wish.

Next call on the totem who is leaving or has left, asking them to join you one last time. They may or may not respond, but you should proceed either way. If you can't think of anything specific to say, softly chant their name for a few moments.

Talk about all the ways in which they've helped you, and thank them for that. Talk about your experiences together and how they changed your life in the time they were with you. If you wish, make a final offering to them and ask if there is anything you can do to honor the memory of your time together (such as taking care of their children, etc.)

Finally, either light a sacred fire or bit of purifying incense, or use a paper, cloth, or feather fan set aside for ritual purposes. Create a trail of smoke or air for the totem to travel on as they continue on their way. Then sweep up the last of their energy, and either send it with them, or place it in one of the statues/pictures/etc. as a keepsake.

Six

Totemism Every Day

Rituals are an important part of many people's spiritual practices. However, they're sometimes the only special occasions in an otherwise mundane life. For some people, the big challenge is making their spirituality an integral part of their everyday experience. While some of the exercises offered in this book encourage you to have daily awareness of the world around you and the totems you work with, this chapter in particular is designed to help you align your spirituality with the rest of your life.

The integration of daily life with spirituality is something I believe is neglected all too often. Spirituality is often treated as something separate from the rest of our lives, a way of thinking that stems in large part from the tendency to see the physical and spiritual as distinctly separate realms. While for the sake of easier teaching I've spoken of the "physical" realm and the "spiritual" realm in meditations and other exercises, I tend to think they gradually blend into one another rather than be sharply divided.

Spirit-body dualists usually see the spiritual as being inherently better or more pure than the physical. Natural processes like the creation of body fluids and the process of death are seen as proof of the corrupt nature of the physical, and the spiritual is held up as some perfect alternate reality in which all the problems of the world are supposedly transcended. Unfortunately, this way of thinking was sometimes used as an excuse to not only neglect the physical world but even actively destroy it—after all, if we have somewhere better to go, why care about this place?

I won't get too far into theology. Suffice it to say that I don't think this old world of ours deserves the abuse we've heaped on it while waiting for some paradise to escape to. In the same vein, I don't see spirituality as something to be relegated to the high holy days or one day a week or even one hour a day. If we combine spirituality with everything else then everything becomes sacred. You're already heading in that direction anyway by practicing totemism; you acknowledge the powerful beings watching over different parts of nature.

But if everything is sacred, why practice spirituality at all? As I mentioned earlier, it's a way to feel connected to something greater than the self, and being able to feel that at any given time in any situation can be incredibly comforting and grounding.

When we feel reverence for something we often want to care for it. The earth and everything on it is in dire need of some TLC, and part of why I present totemism as I do is to invite people to not just take what they want from the totems but also give back and be a healthy part of the community of nature.

In this chapter we'll go over some ways to integrate your totemism into everyday life and begin seeing the sacred all around you. Then we will go into more detail on how to give back to the totems who have helped enrich your experience of life as you've worked with the material in this book.

Hands-on Work

I keep telling you to go outside—and for good reason! Totems are born from the natural history of their physical counterparts, and it's rather pointless to work with totems without having at least some knowledge of the parts of nature they embody. Obviously there are some you may never get close to, such as particularly elusive animals, but you can still appreciate the biotopes they inhabit and the other beings sharing those places.

Most of what you've been doing is simply being outside, observing and exploring places throughout your bioregion as well as meditating and other spiritual work while you're there. There are other ways to connect on a daily basis, and you don't necessarily have to make special trips to do so. What follows are all activities people engage in every day; you might even already be doing some of them. I'd like to tie these activities to totemic work a little more as a way of integrating your spirituality with the rest of your life.

Wildcrafting, Hunting, and Related Quests

These days you probably don't have to look much further for food than the nearest grocery store. But there are still communities around the world where foraging and hunting are central to their way of life, and many other people supplement their diets with wild foods and medicines. These people all maintain a close relationship with the land and its denizens out of necessity and because they appreciate the beauty and splendor of the places from which they draw these resources. It's impossible for nature to remain anonymous when you're immersed in it for your survival.

Wildcrafting is a form of foraging for wild plants, though not necessarily in wilderness settings. A skilled wildcrafter knows what plants (and in some cases fungi) to pick for food, for medicine, for weaving and other crafting materials, and for more specialized purposes. They also know which ones are poisonous or irritating and which ones have parts that are safe while the rest is to be avoided. In an urban environment, the opportunities may be fewer, but even in the city there are green things growing we can gather for more than just decoration.[22]

A hunter captures and kills animals for food and other resources. Hunting is *not* the act of wantonly slaughtering animals for the sake of watching them die. Done correctly, a clean hunt quickly kills an animal that was able to live a wild and free life eating its natural diet, and a responsible hunter makes use of as much of the carcass as they can. One deer can provide

---

22. An excellent book on urban wildcrafting is Rebecca Lerner's *Dandelion Hunter: Foraging the Urban Wilderness.*

meat for a family for weeks, along with bones for nutritional supplements, a hide for clothing, and much more.[23]

Whether you are a hunter, wildcrafter, or both, gathering resources from nature is a good opportunity for totemic work. Even if you're taking from a species whose totem you wouldn't normally work with, there are chances to reach out to them as well as totems of the land itself.

Even if you aren't sure what you'll find once you're on your way, you can speak a general prayer to the totems of your bioregion asking for success. Assure them you won't take more than you need and you'll treat whatever you take with respect. Promise, too, that while you're out you won't do things that harm the soil, water, or air to the best of your ability.

Continue your reverence when you take a plant, animal, or fungus for yourself, particularly if you have to kill it to do so. Make the kill as clean as you can, and thank both the spirit of the living being itself and its totem. Once you're heading back home, give another prayer of gratitude, and again when you're handling the remains of the animal, fungus, or plant you collected. Remember always that in order for you to live, something else must die; I'm not saying this to make you feel guilty but simply to help you not take that fact for granted.

If you aren't sure what to say, here's a good all-purpose prayer you can use or adapt as you see fit:

---

23. Again I refer readers to Miles Olson's excellent book, *The Compassionate Hunter's Guidebook: Hunting From the Heart.*

Totems of the land, sea, and sky, I greet you and I ask you to watch over me this day (night). May I treat your children with the care I would want to be shown myself. May I honor and respect them and their sacrifices, and may I never forget where they came from. Even once I have eaten my fill, created what I need, and stored away the rest, may I always remember I am connected to all things and that none of us are alone in this world. I am grateful for the company.

Gardening

I love to garden. Ever since I moved to the Pacific Northwest I've found ways to grow at least a few plants for food and other purposes, sometimes in planter boxes, sometimes in community garden plots, and once in a swimming pool full of dirt on a neighbor's roof!

Many of the same concepts of wildcrafting and hunting apply to agriculture, particularly regarding treating the plants, animals, and fungi with respect. We carry extra responsibility to the totems' children because we are the ones taking care of them: wild beings can fend for themselves, but cultivated ones rely on us for food, water, shelter, and other needs. We also have a greater and more immediate effect on their living arrangements; we get to choose, for example, whether our small flock of chickens will live in a tiny coop all the time or they'll have access to a larger space in which to roam.[24] We determine whether to augment our garden's soil with caustic chemicals or more organic alternatives. In short, it's about as close as any of us will get to playing God.

Interested in planning a garden with totemism in mind? There are a couple of ways to go about it. You can plant what you would normally plant and then try contacting the corresponding totems as you go along, or you can be more intentional about it, dedicating part of your garden to your totems. Setting an intention doesn't include only planting or otherwise embedding the physical counterparts of plant and fungus totems—it can also mean adding plants that are beneficial to your animal totems' children too. If you're creating a garden from scratch, try not to displace more native species than needed; you may also wish to make apologies and offerings to their totems as well.

If you really want to follow this book's message in a big way, you can even create a microcosm of your bioregion if you have the room in your garden or yard. If your garden is meant to produce food, look into raising some local edibles. Planting native plant and fungus species is a good idea in general; they're more adjusted to the soil and climate where you are, and they provide shelter and food for native animal species. You can turn your yard or porch into a sacred space for totemic work and a haven

---

24. Most of the animals involved in agriculture aren't native species, but were specifically bred for food and other purposes. While I'm mostly focusing on planting native species in the garden, please treat all beings you care for with respect.

for the totems too. It's a lot like creating an outdoor altar of curiosities, only it incorporates living beings. Remember to avoid
adding invasive species; just because a particular plant grows in
your bioregion doesn't mean it's native.

As with wildcrafting and foraging, you can send a prayer
to the appropriate totems before, during, and after the harvest
when harvesting from your garden. Make sure you compost
any leftover stems and other scraps so they can go back into
the soil as well.

Speaking of the soil, it also needs care and upkeep. Most
commercial pesticides, herbicides, fertilizers, and chemicals
are bad for the soil and the things living in and on it. This includes not just beneficial animals like worms and bees but also
the fungi in the soil that help plants absorb nutrients. It's also
true that every time you take away vegetables, fruits, and other
things from the garden, you're taking away nutrients that would
normally return to the soil as the plants died and decayed in the
fall or as native animals digested them and left them as droppings. You'll need to fortify the soil every so often to make up
for that; many good organic alternatives exist. This includes everything from base components like bonemeal and composted
manure to natural fertilizer blends. If you aren't sure what your
soil needs, talk to your local garden shop or greenhouse. You can
even have the soil tested if you want to be extra thorough.

Thank all the totems that help the garden grow, too: Soil
and various mineral totems, Rain, Sun, and the rest. Your salad
isn't a pile of leaves that grew by accident—it's an entire pro-

duction by a cadre of players, all of whom came together in just the right way.

Outdoor Sports and Other Leisure Activities

While some folks may think football is a religion given the fervor of its most devoted fans, it's a little tougher for most of us to see sports as anything other than entertainment. But millions of people make use of parks and other green spaces every day to play sports and games, take walks alone or with companions (human and canine alike), or to simply stretch in the grass and watch the world go by. Other leisure activities are even more nature-oriented; bird-watching, hiking, kayaking, and surfing are just a few of the many things people like to do in the Great Outdoors.

Now some of these activities require more of your direct attention than others and aren't particularly conducive to nature watching. If you're the catcher in a baseball game, your mind's going to be on things besides how the totem Granite is connected to the big blocks of stone that outline the parking lot where you left your car, or wondering whether the grass in the outfield is sprayed with pesticides. And even when it's your turn to sit on the bench while the other team takes the field, you're going to be paying attention to the game. But see if you can find a moment, if not during the game then after, to breathe the air and feel the sun on your skin (or rain, if it's that kind of day) and feel a moment of connection to the land around you.

On the other hand, a lot of outdoor activities are specifically designed to get you more in touch with the land, water, or air. Even the most intense whitewater kayaking trip is about you and the river. While you may have to spend some of your time making sure you don't end up drowning, dropping off a cliff, or getting lost in the woods, there are plenty of opportunities to pause and briefly communicate with the totems where you are. Take a moment to appreciate their physical counterparts and thank them for allowing you a place in their home. Let yourself be awed by the diversity of nature around you.

Keeping open communication with totems becomes easier with practice, too. The more you promote self-awareness of your environment when you're in that environment, the more likely you are to have that awareness even when you're focusing on the activity at hand. Too often we see the outdoors only as the setting for our activities but if we learn to see them as important in and of themselves, too, it enhances our experiences in nature—even if we're also focused on trying to score points for our team.

———

Kevin loves surfing. Ever since he was a young child he loved watching people ride the waves, and once he was old enough to try it out for himself it was as though he was born for it. Every day after school and on weekends and breaks, he'd be out on the beach as much as possible if conditions were right. Even if the ocean wasn't cooperating, he loved to explore the sand and the tidepools and sometimes just watch the waves roll in and out. Now as an adult, Kevin has more responsibilities and misses the freedom he had when he was younger. But he still gets out as much as he can. Few things rejuvenate him like the feeling of the ocean beneath him, supporting him and carrying him along with its power. His very favorite moments are when he's surfing a barrel wave that curls over him in a tunnel; that's when he feels closest to the ocean and for a few moments it's just him and the water, moving as one.

Natural Products In and Outside the Home

We touch nature every single day. As I'm typing this, there's a small cardboard box on my desk. This box is made of fiber from tree trunks—chipped, pulped, flattened, and dried. Even though the fibers have gone through lots of changes, I can still feel the cellulose that gave the wood structure now doing the same for the box. And if you're reading the paperback version of this book, you're also holding what was once a tree.

I couldn't tell you where the trees that gave their cellulose to make this box or your book came from; the same goes for the metals in my computer and the cotton of my shirt. But they all came from bioregions somewhere, and I choose to honor them when I use these products.

Closer to home, I'm a bit of a locavore, preferring food and other products that came from within one hundred miles or so of Portland. The Pacific Northwest has a lot of natural resources as well as many small businesses that make responsible use of them, and I like finding out exactly where in my bioregion these items come from and giving a thank-you to the totems of those places. Since it's what I buy more than anything else these days, it's easiest to stay local with food, and there are some artisans here who make furniture from locally-sourced wood, hand-woven baskets from native plants, and other things I'd also like to purchase as I have the money.

Beyond what we use are some intangibles as well. I am fortunate in that my electric company offers a 100 percent green package, which is mostly composed of hydroelectric power fueled by the Columbia River, along with a smaller amount of local wind energy. So instead of paying for energy from fossil fuels from far-off lands, even the power that's helping me write this book is locally sourced.

Why is all this important to totemism? It's all too easy in our consumption-driven society to take for granted the fact that all the resources we consume have to come from somewhere. Part of my awareness of the origins of the things in my life is connecting with the totems of the beings and phenomena that produced them. The Columbia River is already a central part of my spiritual practice, so I thank the totem River for watching over its children and helping me connect more with both the Columbia and the Willamette. I give gratitude to Soil for the rich dirt that feeds me every time I eat locally grown food and to Rain for the health of this land and its denizens. These totems watch over other rivers and soils and places where the rain falls too, and so they teach me to appreciate other bioregions as well as my own.

You're welcome to add this practice to your life as well. If you aren't sure what local products you're consuming, start with your water. With rare exception, everyone's water comes from within their own bioregion. When you turn on the tap, do you know where your water comes from? And when you watch it flow down the drain, do you know where it goes? If you aren't sure, you can call your water company to find out. Every time you take a shower or wash the dishes or have a glass of water, take a moment to remember your watershed. Thank the totems River and Rain as well as Aquifer if that's where your water comes from. Thanks the totems of the fish and other creatures living in the waterways for sharing their home with you, and thank the plants and animals and other beings that drink from the river for also allowing you to quench your thirst and wash your clothing.

Water's just the start, and it's a good one because it's so universal. Now think: what else in your life can you trace back to your bioregion? What totems watch over the beings that gave of themselves for your food, shelter, clothing, and other possessions? What could you be sourcing more locally while remaining sustainable as well? All these can help you be a more responsible member of your bioregional community, and the totems tend to appreciate this awareness.

Greeting the Neighbors

Remember in chapter 1 when I described some practices for daily awareness? What follows is a similar concept, and you can certainly draw on those practices here. It's quite simple: whenever you're outside surrounded by lawns, gardens, urban trees, wildlife, pets, other animals, and all the other manifestations of nature around you, do your best to acknowledge them as you might notice another human being. You don't necessarily have to walk around saying hello to every blade of grass (that could take a very long time!), but at least take the time to see your fellow beings as more than just the background to your life.

Recall when I talked about plant blindness (the phenomenon of seeing plants only as scenery rather than as active parts of an ecosystem) in chapter 3. Plants are a great starting point for opening up your awareness of the world around you. If you've been making use of the material presented here, you've probably already increased your knowledge of local flora; maybe it's become something of a specialty for you. The real challenge is to make it part of the way you view the world all the time.

The way I started was seeing how many of the plants and fungi I could name while walking around my neighborhood. If I found any I couldn't identify, I took pictures with my camera and looked them up when I got home. While I still don't know the name of every single thing growing around here, knowing some of them has helped me be more conscious of the plants and fungi as individuals, not backdrop.

The concept of familiarity can also be spread out. While the land here has been contoured a bit to allow for development, I can still imagine what it looked like when it was a forest. I watch where the rain falls and where it flows and think of it eventually making it to the Columbia. I am grateful for those neighbors who don't spray their lawns with chemicals and instead are letting the soil recover.

Every instance of this awareness also gets me in touch with the local totems, even if only a little. There have been times where I've called on local totems in situations like asking for help in getting my garden to grow, and having this ongoing relationship of daily greetings made them more amenable to giving me aid. It feels better to live in a place where I can say hi to my neighbors…and not only the human ones.

Bringing It Back to the Human Community

Humans are a part of nature and we shouldn't ever forget it. More than any species on this planet, we are changing the ways ecosystems work, shifting the shape of the land, moving and removing countless species, and doing so in more varied and far-reaching ways than any other force in the history of the planet. We tear open the land like a giant earthquake. We spew gases into the atmosphere like a huge volcano. We chew up other animals like a hunting predator. And like a plague of locusts, we devour all that is before us.

On the other hand, we have the capacity to appreciate and honor the world more than any other species on this planet. Through poetry and other writings, numerous visual media, and the medium of our imagination, we have drawn out countless interpretations of our fellow beings and the places we share. As far as we know, locusts don't recognize the devastation they leave in their wake, but we humans are becoming increasingly aware of the effects of our actions. If a pack of wolves successfully manages to somehow hunt all the elk in a given area, they don't know how to reintroduce their prey; the wolves have to wait for other elk to filter in from elsewhere. We, on the other hand, are seeing what happens when we remove all of a given species from a place. Instead of hoping that another population will fill the void, we actively try to restore balance.

For better or for worse, we are a driving force on the planet. Totemism is a way to reconnect with the nature we are having such massive effects on, and in doing so learning to be more responsible in our actions. If all we do is brag to others that "my totem is such-and-such, I feel *so* enlightened," we are missing a great opportunity to save the very things we claim are sacred. This section addresses some starting points for those wishing to grow their practice in this direction.

Caring for the Human Animal

If we are going to bring the human animal back into the community of nature, we have to treat our own species with as much care as we treat others. We may think we live in a state of luxury and don't need any more pampering, but the sad fact is that we often treat each other pretty terribly. Here in Portland, we have a pretty significant homeless population, and while there are some services to help, they're far from adequate. Most people simply walk by, turning a blind eye to those less fortunate. There are people worldwide made homeless by war, natural disasters, prejudice and bigotry in their communities, and increasingly, the effects of global climate change fueled by our pollutants. And that's just looking at the issue of homelessness and things directly linked to it.

But many of the things harming people also harm the rest of nature, too. Poaching, for example, is often perpetrated by people who believe they have no other options for income or to put food on the table. War eats up huge amounts of resources and leads to a lot of hazardous waste, not just toxic chemicals but also buried land mines; war-torn areas often lead to habitat loss, and the wildlife is often killed or driven away by conflict. Humans do not exist in a vacuum; what we do affects others as well.

Many of the solutions for the environmental challenges we face also address human inequalities as well. Environmental injustice is a concept that demonstrates the disproportionate burden of environmental destruction on poor and otherwise disadvantaged people, among other things. A good example of this is Cancer Alley, the stretch of Mississippi River in Louisiana between Baton Rouge and New Orleans. Not only does it have one of the highest concentrations of industrial plants in the country, but the rate of poverty and proportion of minorities in the population is higher than average. These people are exposed to more toxins in the soil, water, and air than in other areas, and less is being done about it than if residents were more affluent. This sort of pattern repeats itself countless times worldwide, where disempowered people are taken advantage of in the same way as the voiceless land they live on.

While it's ostensibly possible to fix the pollution problem in Cancer Alley and elsewhere without addressing the inequalities, it's that same callousness that allows the abuse of both the people and the land. What can be done? Empowering people is good for the environment on a variety of levels. Recall in chapter 1 where I talked about how helping the environment also helps the people who live on it, particularly since environmental degradation is often heaped upon the poor and marginalized.

As mentioned, poverty often leads people to damage the environment out of sheer desperation through actions like poaching and clearcutting land for agriculture. Communities in which women are educated and have reliable access to birth control have a lower birth rate, easing strain on the land to a greater extent. Even if you're a single-issue activist focused solely on saving the environment, an improved standard of living for the local human community often leads to better treatment of the environment, and so is an important step in environmental activism.

Many of the communities most adversely affected by environmental degradation and other problems are comprised of indigenous people who maintain a connection to the land and its spirits the rest of us have lost and are only now rekindling. We owe these people protection, first and foremost of their persons and their remaining land because it's the right thing to do. Indigenous communities often also carry a great deal of knowledge and wisdom about the land that has all too frequently been ignored in the name of "progress." Had we listened, we might not be in the fix we're in now. Better to listen now than never.

I want to make an important distinction about listening to and respecting the wisdom of indigenous people: we should not attempt to shoehorn our way into their communities just to learn their spiritual secrets and have them teach us to "become one" with the land. Some indigenous cultures are quite private about their religious practices and prefer not to share. Some are more open to sharing, and you should feel fortunate and grateful to be invited to learn from them *not* with a self-centered intent to gain "great power" but to honor the relationships these people have with the land they live on. While the ways in which they relate to the land and its spirits may not be exactly the way it works for you, we can all gain quite a bit by sharing our experiences and working together for the good of all.

––––––

For a few years, Melinda has been working with an organization focused on reintroducing gray wolves to the western United States. They've identified a location near a busy national park that would be ideal with plenty of open spaces and a healthy population of elk, deer, and other prey animals. However, some farmers in the area are concerned about wolf predation. Until about a decade ago, most of the people in the area worked for a local sawmill. When the economy took a downturn, the mill closed and many people lost their jobs. Some of them turned to subsistence farming of crops and cattle to meet as much of their food needs as they could and maybe produce a little extra to sell. They worry that the wolves will prey on their livestock, though some have no real ill will toward the animals. Melinda spends time researching inexpensive and nonlethal ways in which the people could keep wolves away from their stock, and she helps educate them about their options. Her organization convinces the state to put aside a pool of money to reimburse farmers who lose stock to verified wolf kills and drafts a plan to relocate wolves that prey on livestock. Finally, she helps some of the residents draft a plan to create

a tourism industry centered on the wolves and other wild-
life as well as the beauties of the country itself. Five years
later, the reintroduced wolves are thriving. People who
once made money from the mill now lead nature tours and
photography "hunts," and they have built and run a rustic-
themed hotel that opened just outside the park. One en-
terprising local has even started making souvenir plaques
from plaster casts of wolf tracks; "The closest you'll get to
taking one of our wolves home!" she proudly says.

Education and Outreach

While some people already have their own ways of living close to the land, many people especially in more developed countries could use some help in reconnecting. You know how you've been spending a bunch of time getting to know the land you live on and who you share it with? Well, you are now a walking wealth of information, and that's more valuable than you may think! Most people couldn't name ten birds in their neighborhood or explain what a bioregion is, but you can, and you have the opportunity to share that with others.

Mind you, this doesn't mean going door to door and asking people if they have a minute to talk about Our Savior, Lady Gaea! For the most part, people really don't respond well to preaching and proselytization unless they were already halfway to converting anyway. Even people who do go door-to-door on behalf of environmental organizations have to deal with a lot of rejection; I used to work as a field canvasser, and it would be a great night if one in ten people I talked to signed my petition, never mind donated money.

People's resistance or ambivalence doesn't mean there's no opportunity to tell people how awesome you think nature is; it just means you need more tact in knowing when to speak up and when to keep it to yourself. An example of a good opening is when talking with friends or family about current events; sometimes the topic may head in the direction of environmental issues or things tangential to them. Or maybe you're discussing gardening with someone and you are asked about what you do to take care of your garden.

What's even better is to give people opportunities to start the conversation themselves, often by asking questions. We humans learn a lot by watching others, and if you model good behaviors in front of others, they're more likely to be interested. Since I started gardening, I've blogged about my progress and posted pictures online. I don't say "You should be doing this, too!" Instead, I wait for people to ask questions and answer them to the best of my ability, and over the years I've managed to inspire several people to pick up their own gardening efforts again, or even try it for the first time.

It's the same way with totemism. Part of why I write and talk about it so much is so that people who may be interested in the practice know they have someone they can ask about it. I also go into it with the belief that there's no such thing as a stupid question. Everybody has to start somewhere, and sometimes concepts I take for granted are things they had no idea existed. And if they end up deciding it's not for them, I don't try and change their mind.

After all, the goal is not to pressure people into becoming. Instead, all you want to do is give them information. It's up to them what they do with it next. If they decide they want to learn more about organic gardening, or bioregionalism, or working with totems, then do your best to help them get the resources they need to get started.

Group Practice with Bioregional Totemism

Occasionally you may find other people in your area who like your practice enough that they want to emulate it. If you're a solitary practitioner like me, you may be content to share resources (including, if you like, recommending this book to them) and answer their questions. For those spiritual people who like to practice together, what follows are some activities you could do together:

- Go on group outings around the bioregion. If you each have a favorite place, go to one per trip and let the person who suggested it give a tour. You can also introduce the group to the totemic ecosystem there; guided meditation in a group is a good option where the person most connected to the place guides the others through the meditation.

- Meet up every so often to talk about your individual totemic work, compare notes, and provide support to each other. You could even dedicate each meeting to one totem in particular; one person could present their experiences with the totem and the rest of the group could ask questions, share observations, and so forth. The other group members might even try working with that totem and report their results at the next meeting. If the group is so inclined, you can also use these times to do meditations together or even practice group rituals. You might meet once a month, at the solstices and equinoxes, or whenever is convenient. You can also keep in touch more informally in between, in person and online.

- Adopt a park or other place; you can take care of it by cleaning up litter, and removing invasive species and planting native ones if allowed. Check with your state or local department of natural resources or a local environmental group to see if there's an official program to adopt a river, park, or other place. Remember that you're also welcome to do general litter pickup in any public area, even if it isn't "official." Make sure you recycle what you can and safely dispose of the rest.

- As your group becomes more cohesive, you may wish to ask a bioregional totem to be a group guardian. It's better to put a call out and see which totems respond rather than picking one; just because your group thinks a given totem would be a cool symbol for what you're doing doesn't mean they want to be responsible for you. You might try doing a group meditation to see which totems appear for each person and if there's any common ground. Alternately, if you all are in agreement of a totem you'd like as your group guardian, you can respectfully approach that totem and ask if it would like to watch over you. The group totem often protects the members during rituals and other spiritual work but also may work with you individually in between meetings. The totem may also help foster a sense of group unity, representing everything the group stands for.

Keep in mind that your group is meant to be supportive of everyone's work; if you're all going in different directions in your personal practice, that's okay! You don't have to have a single religion shared among everyone. Even if all you do is meet up once a month to have coffee, some small talk, and spend some time discussing your totemic work, that's plenty. Let the group evolve organically.

It's likely that the person or people with the most experience may end up taking more of a leadership role, which doesn't necessarily mean they've become the teacher and everyone else their students. The person with more experience may field more questions because they've been doing this longer. Every member of a group is important, and everyone has the opportunity to teach and learn alike. One thing that helps distribute the responsibility of leading is to have each person be in charge of the meeting for a given month; Person A may lead things for the month of June and talk about environmental news that affects the bioregion, while Person B is in charge of July's meeting and gives a presentation on how to work with the totems of waterways.

Another important thing to keep in mind: your group should not be seen as a recruiting tool. I am not a fan of heavy-handedness, and people do not respond well to being guilted into being more eco-conscious or adhering to a particular spirituality. While some are open and receptive to learning how to be more environmentally friendly, those who aren't will be even less likely to come around if others are trying to shove them down "the good green path." Any group work you do should be for those who are in a good place for it whether that place is ready and raring for more or sort of curious about it. And should someone decide they no longer want to be a part of it, don't be hard on them. Group work isn't for everyone, and sometimes people prefer to go their own way.

———

Anya and Felicia have been practicing bioregional totemism, though Felicia has been practicing for longer. They enjoy sharing ideas with each other and have learned quite a bit that way. They've also been able to show each other places in their bioregion they might not have gone to otherwise, and they sometimes go together to volunteer opportunities offered by the city's parks and recreation department. Their friend Benjamin has recently become curious about all this, and he asks them to help him find out more. Soon Benjamin's girlfriend, Angel, joins them, and it becomes clear that there's more interest in this than Anya and Felicia had first thought. They begin meeting every month at a local bookstore and get permission to put a small flyer on the bulletin board. At first, it's just the four of them, with the occasional curious person looking in, but interest increases after a few months, and they're joined by everyone from neopagans looking for a more nature-based spirituality to environmentalists wanting to understand their bioregion better. Even a retired biology professor from the local community college attends their meeting. Some only stay for one meeting, while others show up regularly. Even with all this momentum, Anya and Felicia still make time to go out together, and other group members often engage in smaller-scale activities on their own. The monthly meeting becomes an introduction that allows attendees to figure out their own best paths.

Giving Back to the Totems

Throughout these pages I have emphasized that totemism—especially bioregional totemism—is a two-way street. It is not solely reliant on what the other denizens of the world (physical and otherwise) can do for us; we are instead encouraged to reintegrate ourselves into the ecosystems of which we are a part. What I present in this book is not the One True Path of Connecting to Nature. It is an invitation to have a more complete series of multilayered relationships with the beings and phenomena around us.

Too often with animal, plant, and fungus totems we focus too heavily on what they can do for us and what we can get from them. There's nothing wrong with asking for help or learning new perspectives. But as with so much about modern-day culture, there's a decided self-centeredness to it. Animal totems do not exist only to impart great wisdom upon us. Plant and fungus totems are not around just to help us heal other humans or experience psychoactive trips. Land totems do not just preside over our construction projects.

Bioregional totemism isn't a way to approach several layers of totemism at once. Think of it as a more systemic approach to being an inhabitant of the Earth, taking our anthropocentric tendencies down a few notches (without making us feel guilty for being human), while increasing our awareness of our wider community in addition to the actions resulting from that awareness. If you think of anthropocentric awareness and bioregional awareness as being on the ends of a continuum, the bioregional totemic approach helps slide our location further toward the bioregional end.

How, then, do we give back to the totems and their children who have given us so much? Think about what you might do for another human being who has helped you out. You might take them out to eat, give them a card or gift, or tell them in detail why you appreciate what they did for you. If they ask you for a favor later on, you'll probably be even more motivated to help them than before, assuming it's something you're able to do.

Of course, you can't go to the local card shop and get a "Thank you, totems!" card, but there are many ways to show your appreciation for the totems and their kin. Here are some of my favorites.

Volunteering and Donations

I have to admit that volunteering time and making financial donations to environmental nonprofit groups is probably my favorite offering of all. A list of some of my personal favorite organizations appears in Appendix B.

Volunteering is a great option for many people because it doesn't require you to spend anything other than whatever it costs to get to the volunteer site. Most organizations have a variety of things requiring help: tree planting, litter pickup, and other outdoor activities are popular, but if you're physically incapable of participating in this way, you may be able to help with something more low-impact like clerical work or envelope stuffing. If you like talking to people, some organizations have information tables at street fairs and other events and need a few volunteers to staff it.

You don't necessarily have to volunteer under the aegis of an official organization. Going around your neighborhood and picking up trash does plenty, and cleaning up litter in places where others may see you shows them that someone cares. Hopefully it makes potential litterbugs more likely to think twice before tossing a cigarette butt or empty cup in the gutter. All the trash you pick up is trash that won't get washed into the storm sewer and from there into the rivers and ocean.

If you have more money to spare than time, consider giving some to the environmental nonprofit of your choice. Donations are important because you're giving more resources to people who may be able to do work you're not able to, like lobbying for lawmakers and organizing reintroduction efforts for endangered species. You don't have to make huge, three- and four-figure donations to be effective—often it's just a matter of choosing to spend your money a little differently. Instead of buying a t-shirt with a wolf on it or a stuffed toy walrus, put the money toward groups that protect wolves and walruses. Keep in mind that even if an organization offers you a shirt, tote bag, or other souvenir as incentive to donate, you can refuse it and let them keep the money it cost them to obtain that prize in the first place.

If you really want to combine the two forces, volunteer to do some fundraising. Your contribution can be as simple as holding a yard sale maybe with the help of a few friends, and donating the proceeds to the organization of your choice. Another option is asking the organization if you can put together something more elaborate like an art auction or a fundraising night at a local restaurant.

Physical Offerings

Just as there are no totemic greeting cards, there aren't totems with post office boxes to receive them. That doesn't mean you can't make or buy a gift for your totems—you just have to be a little more creative in how you get it to them.

Let's say you're in a thrift store and you see a statue of a seagull that reminds you very strongly of one of your totems, Herring Gull. You buy it, but now what do you do with it? If you leave it by the water where the gulls congregate, at most they're going to poop on it until someone decides to throw it out or it gets carried away by a wave. Why not take it home and add it to your altar of curiosities, or even start a new one that's made of nothing but offerings to your totems? These make especially good "guest rooms" for the totems when they're visiting because it's something you acquired especially for them.

That statue could be a good place for Herring Gull to stay in your home.

Maybe you don't have a lot of space in your home for knickknacks, even if they are spiritually oriented, but you can't bear to leave that absolutely perfect statue behind. One possible way to move it on to a new home is to sell it in a fundraiser for a nonprofit that benefits the gulls, perhaps a group that cleans up litter along the beach or advocates for maintaining wild, undeveloped coastline. If the statue itself isn't all that impressive by most people's standards and you feel up to a creative project, you could incorporate it into a more elaborate piece of artwork. Or you could take it around to different places where herring gulls can be found and take pictures of the statue there to raise awareness of the gulls and their habitat and then sell the statue with a set of prints to raise money for the group. The organization might even have some ideas to help you with your fundraising, too.

An alternate (and less involved) idea is giving the gift of Gull energy. In this case, think of someone who might benefit from meeting Herring Gull. Maybe you know someone else who works with totems and is fairly new to the concept. You could use the statue as a way of introducing this person to Herring Gull and providing him or her a way to start working together. You may wish to ask Herring Gull for permission before doing this and also allow your friend the ability to say "thanks but no thanks" as well. It may just work out that you've managed to offer Herring Gull a new ally.

Some of you may be asking, "Why not buy some fries at a fast food place and give them to the gulls as an offering?" It does sound pretty easy, given that gulls are notorious scavengers of human detritus. However, just because gulls eat our leftovers doesn't mean it's good for them.

For one thing, we eat a lot of things that aren't particularly good for wildlife. (To be fair, some of those things aren't exactly healthy for us, either.) People like to feed bread to ducks and geese at park ponds without realizing that there's very little nutritional value in it for them. The ducks and geese fill up on the bread and then don't eat food that actually nourishes them which makes them sick, malnourished, and can even lead to permanent deformation of their wings.[25] Feeding wildlife no matter the species also makes them more dependent on humans for food, which can lead them to stop looking for natural sources of food. It puts them in greater proximity to humans, which can lead to them getting hit by cars, attacked by dogs, shot by humans, getting into garbage cans and gardens, and having to be relocated or killed as nuisances—in short, it just doesn't go very well for the wildlife. While there are exceptions—in the United Kingdom, for example, many wild bird species are threatened enough by extinction that backyard feeders are invaluable in preserving the populations that remain—as a general rule, giving food to your totem's physical counterparts isn't a good idea. There are other ways to offer food, however. As mentioned earlier, you can grow plants

---

25. Yes, really. Check out the article at https://my.spokanecity.org/news /stories/2014/04/08/dont-feed-the-ducks/ for more information.

and fungi that support local wildlife if you have a garden or yard; try planting red honeysuckle or red trumpet vine (after making sure you can keep them contained if they aren't native to your area) instead of a hummingbird feeder if you want to make offerings to Anna's Hummingbird. Even if your totem doesn't directly benefit from what you plant, having native species around to support local pollinators and other creatures is good for the ecosystem and everyone in it.

My favorite way to offer food to my totems is to have a picnic with them. I pack up a lunch and head out to one of my power spots or other appropriate location, or I formally invite them into my home. I lay out food with a prayer of thanks to the beings whose remains I am about to eat, and then I invite the totems to partake of the spiritual essence of the food. Once they've had their fill, I eat the food and thereby have the benefit of the physical nutrients. (And so betwixt us both, you see, we lick the platter clean.)

Rituals

For some totems, a ritual celebrating your bond is a wonderful offering indeed—we humans aren't the only ones who like to feel appreciated. So take some time out to create a sacred space and time where you show your gratitude to the totems that have helped you, and perhaps tell others about their generosity, too.

Rituals can also be used to augment other offerings. When I was talking about using your bioregional map for ritual work, I mentioned letting the map represent a place you're trying to protect and doing a ritual to add the totems' energy to your efforts to protect the place. A ritual can also be a rallying point for you and other volunteers to get motivated just before digging into a patch of invasive species or collecting signatures on a petition to support an eco-friendly law. And if you do turn that gull statue into an amazing work of art to sell, you can do a ritual of blessing before sending it on its way.

———

Marcus is going to a protest a local environmental group is organizing against a coal company that wants to remove the tops of several local mountains to mine the coal inside them. The children of one of his totems, Black Bear, live on and around these mountains and would be driven out of their habitat by the mining. Marcus wants to dedicate his efforts to Black Bear and the bears themselves. He clears out a space in his home where he intends to make the sign he'll hold during the protest. He lays out on the floor his posterboard and markers, a statue of a black bear dedicated to his totem, and a bowl of honey. He asks Black Bear to watch over him and invites the totem to partake of the spiritual essence of the honey. Then he quiets his mind, and as he writes out his message on his sign, he thinks of all the black bears on the mountains and how he wants to keep them safe. In one corner of the sign he draws a bear on top of a mountain with a red circle around it to protect it. When he is finished, he eats the honey and says, "Let this honey give me strength today as I fight for you, and let me have a victory as sweet as this food." Then he takes his sign and heads out to meet the rest of the protestors.

Living Green

This chapter is about ways to make bioregional totemism a part of everyday life. For me personally, a big part of that is living in such a way that minimizes my effect on my bioregion as much as possible. I live in a small apartment rather than a big house; I drive a car with good mileage and a roof rack instead of a gas-guzzling SUV, and I try to walk or take public transit when I can. I garden and buy organic and free-range food when I can afford it. Most of my possessions are secondhand, and when I get rid of something I find the best place to donate it, or leave it on the curb in a "free box." I make art with a lot of reclaimed materials and donate part of the money to environmental nonprofits. And yes, I'll donate a bit of the money from this book, too.

The common theme here is that all these things fit within my schedule and financial means. What living green means to me may be different for someone with enough money to buy a house and retrofit it with solar power or buy an electric car. It's also different from what someone may be able to do if they're trying to support a family of five on one income, are only living on social security, or have a significant disability. If you want to live a greener life, decide how you'll show the totems that you're invested in protecting the home you both share, even if you can only make a few small changes right now.

You may need to do a little research to see what your options are; for example, you may never have considered where the electricity in your home comes from or if it's derived from fossil fuels or greener sources. A quick call to your electric company should get you some answers. If they offer a renewable energy option, get an estimate of how much more your bill is likely to be if you switch and determine whether this is in your budget.

When it comes to making green choices, there's often debate as to which is the best. Should you use your dishwasher because it ultimately uses less water, or wash the dishes by hand because it doesn't use electricity? Do you buy a brand new desk made of bamboo grown in a plantation, or a secondhand wooden one? And which is really better: paper or plastic—or are reusable bags better than both? Be wary of greenwashing, where a product, service, or company that's supposedly eco-friendly really isn't. Some bigger household chemical companies have produced "greener" cleaning products as specialty items but still make most of their money on harsher, traditional chemicals.

Specialty "green" items can get pretty expensive, as companies know some people are willing to pay more for a supposedly eco-friendly option. Would you believe that some of the best alternatives are the cheapest? Continuing with cleaning products, one of the best household disinfectants and all-around cleaning solutions is a 50-50 blend of water and white vinegar. Baking soda is as good an abrasive as any, and old clothes make excellent cleaning rags that save you money on paper towels. As for secondhand items, they are almost always cheaper than new ones; I once restocked my kitchen at a thrift store and spent less than $50 on the dishes and other cookware

I needed. Oftentimes what's better for the earth is also better for your wallet.

There will always be someone disagreeing with your green choices, even those who also want to be better to the earth. It can be overwhelming at times, and sometimes it does feel a bit like a part-time job trying to stay on top of the latest news and information. As with all things, do the best you can with what you have, and adapt as you find better solutions. It's best if your efforts to live green are a means to feel like a better part of your bioregional community, not a big source of stress. The totems will appreciate whatever effort you're able to put forth.

———

Really, whatever efforts you can make to help the totems is what this entire chapter (and book) are about. I'm giving you a toolkit you can use as you see fit, but you're the only person who can determine the best ways to incorporate your totemism in your life. If there are things here you like, run with them. If you want to adapt them, change what you need to. And if they spark new ideas in your mind, go ahead and give them a try. The most important thing is that they work; the rest is details.

Conclusion

Wonder and Awe
at the World

I wrote this book entirely on computers, primarily Selina, my desktop, and my laptop, Columbia. For someone who loves the outdoors as much as I do, I spend an awful lot of time staring at the screen, but that's part of the price I pay for the role I play in society as a writer, artist, and would-be advocate for environmental causes. I grew up with computers; they're an integral part of my understanding of the world I inhabit, just like nonhuman nature. With the ever-expanding importance of the Internet as a mode of communication and exchange of ideas, I can't do my job if I disconnect entirely.

There's a reward for the strain I sometimes feel when I've been sitting at the desk too long, trying to tease out just the right words from my brain to the pixels on the screen. Even when I am most deeply immersed in technology, I am connected to the world around me. From the background photo on my desktop to the logo for my website, I've placed little reminders of non-human nature all around my workspace, physical and virtual. These reminders assure me that once I've put the last few words down and get to take a break, there's a whole big world out there waiting for me. When break time comes, I step out the apartment door. Sometimes I'm greeted by raindrops pattering on the landing, soaking into the worn Astroturf and pinging off the metal railing. Other times, I walk down the stairs to a street bathed in broad sunlight. When I open the door at night, it's positioned just so that I can see the moon rise if the timing's right and the clouds cooperate.

I walk down the street, and depending on the time of day or night I might see scrub jays in the cherry branches and on the power lines, or a raccoon ambling across the street to nose at another garbage can. In spring I smell the rhododendron blossoms that lay against the siding of old houses, and I keep my eyes peeled for black morels popping up out of patches of mulch. A couple walks by so engrossed in each other that they barely notice me, never mind the brown rat foraging in the grass just a few feet away. Occasionally I am treated to my favorite nighttime sky, deep midnight blue with pale white clouds overhead.

All of these are quite ordinary, and yet they are what I find so extraordinary about this world. It's not just the pretty colors of the flowers or sweet songs of the birds that get to me. It's that they exist in the first place and how they got to be here that truly moves me. The more I understand of the workings of the world, the more precious and beautiful and fragile it all seems. Photosynthesis is a miracle, eating is a sacrament, and the Big Bang is the greatest mystery that we're untangling with every new discovery.

I got into totemism and animal magic almost twenty years ago because I was that kid who loved animals, and finding a spiritual path that centered on them seemed to be exactly what I needed. But it took several years for me to figure out why I needed it. I spent a long time trying to find "the way," sometimes engaging in ever more complex devotional regimens in the hopes of being pious enough, other times exploding my entire practice to smithereens and starting all over. It wasn't until I stopped trying so hard and just went outside more that I finally returned to what had first fed me when I was young: wonder and awe.

We use these words all the time, but what do they really mean? *Wonder* is to think about, to consider; we wonder about something that prompts us to want to know more. To be *awed* is to be overwhelmed by something, not in a horribly terrifying manner but in a sense of deep reverence and appreciation (and maybe a little healthy amount of fear depending on the situation). Wonder leads me to explore trails and crannies and see where they lead, and awe is what I feel when I am so immersed in what I find that I can't contain how I feel.

Many of us are so overstimulated by our environments that we've become numb to all but the loudest, fastest, and most intense sensory input. For some, the first step to reclaiming our sense of wonder and awe will be learning to be open to the world again not in its artificially amped-up forms but in the way it really is. It may take some time and patience but all is not lost; we can learn to appreciate the things we have taken for granted.

The totems are our allies in the reclamation process. They are not simple one-dimensional helpers limited to stereotyped meanings from dictionaries. They are vibrant, intelligent, dynamic beings sharing the world with us as much as anyone else, and while we may have forgotten what it is to be in nature's community, they have not. They're still waiting with their physical counterparts in the land and water and skies, holding a place for us to return to, and I am grateful to them for that. They helped to reawaken in me my wonder and awe, the tiny flame put into me when I was first born into this world and all was new to me.

If I could give nothing else to my readers, no other lesson or piece of wisdom or spiritual tool, it would be the feeling that everything in our world is amazing, worthy of exploration and preservation. That "worth" is not defined in terms of our selfish needs—simply, it exists. I would give everyone an understanding of the universe's intrinsic value and not one iota less.

I invite you to talk to the totems. Ask them what they would show you, if you would only look and listen. Be open, be interested, and be curious.

Good paths to you.

Appendix A:
Recommended Reading

While it would be easy for me to say "read my other books" and leave you with that, there are titles by other authors you may wish to look into as complements to the material in this book. They're not all necessarily focused on totemism, or even on spirituality, but they're all books that in one way or another mesh with what I've shared here.

In addition to the following books, I also recommend picking up a good field guide or two outlining the flora, fauna, and fungi of your bioregion, as well as at least one good book on its geological history. If you can find material on the local or regional climate and weather patterns, add that to your bookshelf as well.

Ecoshamanism: Sacred Practices of Unity, Power, and Earth Healing by James Endredy: I was fortunate enough to receive a bit of training from James a few years ago, and if I were going to hand people anything as a workbook for deepening their relationship with their bioregion, this would be it. If you enjoyed the exercises in this book, *Ecoshamanism* should be high on your to-read-next list.

The Earth Path: Grounding Your Spirit in the Rhythms of Nature by Starhawk: This is a great book for shaking people out of purely symbolic approaches to the four classic elements: earth, air, fire, and water. Through essays and meditations, Starhawk ties the elements to their physical sources not in an academic sense, but by illustrating our interactions with them every day, even those we don't give active attention.

The Nature Principle: Reconnecting with Life in a Virtual Age and *Last Child in the Woods: Saving Our Children from Nature-Deficit Disorder*, both by Richard Louv: A journalist and avid environmentalist, Louv makes very salient arguments on why nature is good for all of us, old and young alike, not just for sentimental reasons, but because the deprivation of time in nonhuman nature has some seriously negative effects on us. He's not all doom and gloom, however; constructive and reasonable solutions to the problems are also addressed.

Green Metropolis: Why Living Smaller, Living Closer, and Driving Less Are the Keys to Sustainability by David Owen: I've met a lot of Pagans and other eco-friendly people who fantasize about buying land somewhere to create their own little eco-communities, vilifying cities as cesspits of filth and devoid of nature. I offer this particular book as a good counter to that attitude and assumption, and it serves as a great pool of ideas for all of us green folk who live in urban areas whether by necessity or choice.

Coming Back to Life: The Updated Guide to the Work that Reconnects by Joanna Macy and Molly Young Brown: This book is full to overflowing with meditations and rituals that not only help us to reconnect with nonhuman nature, but to each other as well. Macy is especially known for her work in creating spaces to grieve for the environment and the world as a whole, and some of the exercises in this book are wonderful for working through despair and overwhelmingness in the face of our many challenges.

You'll notice I haven't included any totem dictionaries in here. After spending a couple of hundred pages encouraging you to make your own relationships with the totems, I'm not eager to point you toward what would be spoon-fed instant answers. If you must make use of books with "this animal means that" entries, remember that they are limited by their authors' knowledge and biases as well as whatever a given totem tells the author—it may not be what a totem wants to tell you.

Appendix B:
Beneficial Nonprofit Organizations

There are a lot of worthy environmental nonprofits out there. The following are some of my favorites for donations. Keep in mind these are large national and international organizations. You likely also have more local groups doing a lot of boots-on-the-ground work for your bioregion, so consider helping them with a donation and/or volunteer time.

The Millennium Seed Bank
Project at the Kew Gardens

Wakehurst (Wakehurst Place and Millennium Seed Bank)
Ardinglynr Haywards Heath
West Sussex
RH17 6TN
United Kingdom
+44 (0)20 8332 5000

wakehurst@kew.org

kew.org/science-conservation/millennium-seed
-bank

The largest seed bank in the world, working to preserve some of the most endangered plant species in the world. The Kew Gardens also maintains a sizeable selection of fungal samples, to include spores.

Seed Savers

3094 North Winn Rd.

Decorah, IA 52101

USA

(563) 382-5990

www.seedsavers.org/

Since 1975, Seed Savers has not only worked to preserve heirloom seeds, but also provides seeds for sale. They offer a membership package with a variety of horticultural and educational benefits.

The Nature Conservancy

4245 North Fairfax Drive, Suite 100

Arlington, VA 22203-1606

USA

(800) 628-6860

www.nature.org

The Nature Conservancy focuses on protecting habitats around the world and educating people about the importance of healthy ecosystems. This includes direct protection of individual habitats in conjunction with local communities.

The Ocean Conservancy

1300 19th Street, NW
8th Floor
Washington, DC 20036
USA
(800) 519-1541
www.oceanconservancy.org

Works to protect the world's oceans and create awareness of how crucial the oceans and their inhabitants are to the planet's health as a whole.

The Sierra Club

85 Second Street, 2nd Floor
San Francisco, CA 94105
USA
Phone: (415) 977-5500
www.sierraclub.org

One of the oldest and largest environmental nonprofits, the Sierra Club combines government lobbying with grassroots organization for a variety of ecological causes.

Natural Resources Defense Council

40 West 20th Street
New York, NY 10011
USA
(212) 727-2700
www.nrdc.org

Lobbies for the protection of both wild species and their environments, and is also instrumental in helping communities become more sustainable.

The Wilderness Society

1615 M St., NW
Washington, DC 20036
USA
(800) THE-WILD
www.wilderness.org

Many plants and fungi that face extinction are vulnerable due to habitat loss; the Wilderness Society works to preserve wilderness areas to include crucial habitat.

Appendix C:
Helpful Hints for Totemic Research

One of the key components of bioregional totemism is physical nature itself. Your personal spiritual experiences are definitely important, particularly when it comes to understanding your relationship with the land you live on and the beings you share it with. There's also great value in more collective knowledge about nature through the natural sciences, firsthand accounts, and other third-party information.

The sheer volume of information available about even a single bioregion can be overwhelming. You may wish to keep notes and other important information in a three-ring binder or a file on your computer. I personally find it useful to keep a collection of commercially published field guides about living beings, geological formations, and other natural phenomena in my own bioregion for quick reference.

Natural History

Natural history is the direct observation of living beings and other natural phenomena. All the natural sciences, from biology to astronomy to geology, rely heavily on natural history to understand the subjects being studied. While laboratory research and theories are certainly important, you don't need to have a thorough understanding of, say, the chemical composition of a quartz crystal in order to know the basic forces that formed it.

There are plenty of ways to use natural history to enhance your spiritual path. Let's say one of your local totems is Snail Darter, the totem of a little fish found in streams in certain parts of the American southeast. If you're able, you could go and directly observe these fish in their native homes and perhaps even trace their migratory route to ancestral spawning grounds. If there's a state or national park nearby, the ranger station or learning center may have information on snail darters; the same goes for natural history museums in the area.

Don't forget your local library as a resource as well. In the example of Snail Darter above, you could visit the library and see what books they have on snail darters and their habitats. This fish is an endangered species and was at the center of a big environmental controversy in the 1970s and 1980s when a proposed dam threatened its habitat. The library might have microfilm or microfiche of the original newspaper articles, and some may be found online as well. This is a great opportunity to find out more about other people's relationships to totems (in this case snail darters) and the ecosystems they're part of, including *why* some wanted to make sure these species were saved from extinction. If any of the activists who helped protect the snail darter are still around, you could ask the librarian if they've given any recent interviews about their experiences.

There's only so much to know about the snail darter itself — it eats snails and other small invertebrates, prefers to hang out at the bottom of clear streams, and makes relatively short migrations to spawn in quiet pools. But what makes a stream good snail darter habitat, and how was it formed in the first place? How common are the fish's food sources, and what are the life cycles of the animals it feeds on? Does it become food in turn for larger predators, who are then preyed upon by still larger animals? How do the plants and fungi in and around the stream help maintain its quality? These are just a few of the questions you could ask once you start looking past the little fish itself.

To find the answers, you could delve more deeply into your reading both online and in books and magazines. Many natural history museums feature exhibits that explain how local ecosystems are formed and what lives there; these displays are often more accessible, especially for people of limited mobility or who may not have the time or resources to head out into wild places to watch snail darters in their homes. If you do well in a classroom setting, you may want to check the nearest community college for classes on local ecosystems or related topics. Additionally, environmental groups like the Audubon Society may offer workshops that are often free to the public or accessible for a small fee. Park rangers are generally pretty well-educated on the natural history of the places they watch over, so if you head to the ranger station or learning center, you'll likely be able to get some answers to your questions or at least good leads on more information.

Mythology and Folklore

Humans have always enjoyed observing their world and telling stories about what they see. While there's nothing wrong with a straightforward description of one's experiences, many people consider it to be more fun when a tale is involved. Over time the body of stories grows into a cohesive mythos shared by a culture or community, passed down from generation to generation.

I am not native to the Portland area. However, the various communities of the Chinookan people have lived along the Columbia River for centuries. There are no snail darters here but we do have several species of salmon, and I've spoken with the totems of a couple of them. It would be short-sighted of me to ignore the historical relationships the Chinookan people have had with the salmon, as well as the myths they've created for them. This helps me understand the salmon more, their place in the Columbia and surrounding rivers, and their importance to all who live here, human and otherwise.

Salmon are fairly high-profile critters, and it's relatively easy to find information about them and their myths. The snail darter seems to not have a single historical tale of its own, though it certainly made an impact in more recent years. If the totem you're researching isn't the subject of easily accessible myths, start reading up on the myths and folklore of the indigenous people of its land. Even if you don't find a word about your totem, you'll gain valuable lore about the place it lives and other beings it calls neighbors.

Do be aware that on occasion folklore can be fraught with tragic inaccuracies. All surviving rhinoceros species are very close to extinction because certain Chinese medicine traditions claim that rhino horn has medicinal powers. None of these qualities have been verified by science, yet their persistence has led to the widescale poaching of rhinos and the extinction of multiple subspecies thereof. In a similar vein, medieval European lore claims that salamanders can live in fire, all because Pliny the Elder said so in his writings. If you toss a real salamander into a fire, the poor thing will die horribly just as you or I would under the same circumstances. Remember: just because something has been claimed for a long time doesn't mean it's true.

A final note: since the industrial age gained traction in the nineteenth century, a new sort of mythos has risen to counter its destructive tendencies. Nature writing is a form of nonfiction that reflects on the natural world most often through prose (though observations and experiences may also be conveyed as poetry). Some of the best-known classic American nature writers include Henry David Thoreau, Aldo Leopold, and John Muir. More recent contributors to the field are Terry Tempest Williams, Jane Goodall, and Thomas Berry. The stories these writers tell are largely based in observation and the physical world; some writers such as Goodall have extensive scientific training and expertise. Like older myths, their writings capture a certain spirit about their subjects which speaks to both the beings they write about and those species' totems. An idea does not need to be expressly spiritual in order to be inspiring.

Personal Observations

Journaling has been a popular tool with naturalists and spiritual people alike for a very long time—there are a lot of things to record!

Returning to those snail darters, suppose you were able to visit their stream at least once a week for an hour. It may seem a bit tedious to sit and watch little fish, and it might be hard to concentrate at first. But the more you watch them, the more you're likely to notice what makes them unique. You may get to see them feeding on prey and make note of what they commonly eat. Or you could follow their migratory progress to their spawning pools, and keep an eye out for newly hatched fish in the days and weeks to come. As you observe other species in the water, you'll get a clearer idea of the place the snail darters have in their community.

Even if you can't visit the stream every day, you can keep track of more general observations. A few good starters are noting when the sun and moon rise and set; daily rainfall, temperatures, and other weather patterns; any animals you may notice outside your home; what the plants and fungi are doing during this time of the year; your body's responses to seasonal changes like light, allergens, temperatures, and so on; and human activity in your neighborhood. Over time you may notice patterns and will likely find yourself more attuned to your environment in general. Then when you are able to go see the snail darters (or whatever other beings you're observing) you'll be more prepared to catch little details you may have missed before, details that can tell you more about them.

These journal entries are also useful in working with totems. We often consider the big, impressive mammalian and avian predators like wolves and eagles to be the best teachers of hunting skills, courage, and cunning. However, the snail darter is no weakling in its own home. What strategies do snail darters have in catching their prey, and what could the totem Snail Darter teach you as a result? Perhaps you'd learn about how to carefully seek out opportunities that may be hidden, just as snail darters can find snails camouflaged among the gravel in the stream bed. Or maybe Snail Darter will remind you that sometimes we have to leave the comfort of familiar territory to achieve greater success, just as snail darters move from their usual haunts to bring forth the next generation.

As with everything presented here, don't worry about creating a professional-level journal. You don't need to have scientifically accurate sketches in your entries; you don't even have to write in complete sentences, so long as you can go back and read what you wrote and still be able to understand it. So get creative! Write or draw whatever strikes you as important in the moment, and go back and add to it later after you've had some time to reflect. Paste in pictures of relevant animals, plants, and other beings from magazines, Wikipedia, and other sources. If you're using a binder, cut or print out articles that add to your observations, or have fellow naturalists write their own thoughts on a blank page. These are just a few of the ways you can use your journal—and they're hardly the limit.

Don't forget the bioregional map from chapter 2. If that particular tool really works for you, use it in conjunction with (or even instead of) a journal. You might use the journal to record your thoughts about the map, or to further explain why you highlighted certain portions. You could also number each journal entry, and then put the same number on the place(s) you wrote about in that entry.

Online Resources

The Cornell Lab of Ornithology's site at www.allaboutbirds .org, features field marks (appearance, song, etc.) for hundreds of species of North American birds. The database at avibase .bsc-eoc.org/avibase.jsp doesn't have nearly as many features as Cornell's, but it does include birds from around the world. If you're looking for a great community to help you in those times when you can't find any information on a particular bird of which you have a photograph, check out www.reddit .com/r/whatsthisbird.

Need help identifying a tree? trees.luidp.net/en/index.php doesn't have every single species, but it's a great start, particularly in teaching you what characteristics to look for (bark, leaf shape and size, etc.) www.reddit.com/r/whatsthisplant is also good for "I have this picture, what is it?"-type identification of plants.

Want to study the stars? Try neave.com/planetarium/ and www.skymaponline.net/ to find out which constellations are overhead at any given time.

www.peakfinder.org/ is one of my very favorite sites. Put in GPS coordinates and it'll tell you the names of all peaks and hills you can see in a 360 degree panorama, assuming they have names.

Want to figure out what your watershed is when all you have is a topographic map? www.wvca.us/envirothon/pdf /Watershed_Delineation_2.pdf has great directions.

Appendix D:
A Quick Guide to Guided Meditation

As you may have noticed, this book relies heavily on guided meditation. The purpose of a guided meditation is to use visual imagery or other sensory cues to help you reach a more relaxed altered state of consciousness where you can access a sort of "other realm" where the totems may meet you. From a purely psychological perspective, it allows you to access other layers of your consciousness besides your normal state of awareness. In this altered state you can explore possibilities not accessible in everyday life. We're not going to see a totem walking down the street; that crow you see on the phone line is just that—a crow. It may have a connection to the totem Common Crow, but it's not the totem in and of itself. In our meditations we can see and talk with the totems however they choose to present themselves.

If you don't have a lot of experience with this practice, try some of the tips and techniques in this appendix to help you hone your skills. Extra practice is especially important if think your inexperience may interfere with your ability to do some of the exercises in this book or if you've already been having trouble with them.

General meditation improvement

Sometimes it's best to start with the basic skills you'll need for all sorts of meditation: focus, patience, and relaxation. Focus is what helps you to stay embedded in your meditation. Early on you may need to get rid of all distractions—sitting in a quiet room where no one will disturb you for a while, for example. With more practice you may be able to focus on your meditation even if the neighbors are yelling or you're a little too cold or your stomach's rumbling. Patience allows you to stay put for longer periods and to keep trying with meditation even when you feel frustrated with your (lack of) progress. Relaxation allows you to let go of other concerns for the moment, like what to make for supper or a bad experience at work. It also helps your body to calm down and stop releasing the natural chemicals and hormones that may keep you too keyed up and alert to tiny distractions.

There are countless guides to meditation in book and online form, and there are classes in most metropolitan areas. Think of how you learn best—are you more of a self-teacher armed with books and other materials, or do you prefer the guidance of other people to support your efforts? Try different methods of basic meditation; some rely on complete stillness and a quiet mind while others require you to maintain your focus on a single chant or image. It will take time to figure out which methods work best for you. Above all, remember to be patient with yourself. It takes most people years to get good at meditation.

Scripted, guided meditations

My guided meditations tend to allow you a lot of freedom. Some people find themselves a bit lost once we get past the part where I tell you where to go and what to look for; the free-form part of the meditation is often the toughest. Often people may tell me after the meditation that they found themselves wandering off the path and instead of finding a totem they simply walked in circles, or ended up meditating on something not related to totemism at all. Or they may find a possible totem but not be able to communicate it, or have it fade in and out of the meditation.

A lack of focus is the biggest cause of this phenomenon. Think of it like having weak phone reception; the message is there, but it's hard to get through the static. One of the best ways to get better at focusing in the altered state of guided meditation is to practice with fully scripted meditations first. These are the ones that tell you what to do from start to finish. I don't recommend them for totemic work simply because the author of the meditation is already dictating which totem you'll find, what they'll tell you, etc. But they're great preparation for the more free-form meditations I advocate in totemism.

One of my favorite sets of basic guided meditations to practice with can be found at http://marc.ucla.edu/body.cfm?id=22.

These are more focused on your awareness of your body, but they're excellent for helping you stay focused up to twenty minutes at a time. For those wanting more of a story format, I recommend Nicki Scully's *Power Animal Meditations* (Bear & Company, 2001); all the meditations are fully scripted and help prepare you for the sort of experiences you may have in more free-form guided meditations.

Some people like to record themselves reading the meditation scripts out loud and then meditate while playing the recordings, or have someone else read for them. Others prefer to memorize the scripts and then meditate from memory. Whatever method works best for you is the one you should use.

I am hard of hearing and can't hear the meditation recordings/I have trouble with visualization or other sight-based exercises

One of the shortcomings of guided meditation is that it assumes certain sensory preferences. If you can't hear a recorded or live-read meditation, you will need to find another alternative. For some who have no hearing at all, this may be memorizing the meditation and playing it back in their head. For others, it may be more useful to have the words up on a computer screen or open book, though this may make having a visual meditation more challenging as they switch between what their physical eyes see and what their inner eyes see. Similarly, if you are blind you may need the meditation printed into Braille, and again either memorize it or read it as you go through the meditation with the same potential challenges between paying attention to what you're reading and trying to imagine.

Sight is the most common sense invoked in guided meditation. Most meditations ask you to "see" yourself walking down a path and "look" at various things in your meditation. For some people, that just won't work. If you cannot visualize in your head no matter how hard you try or if you have been blind for long enough that you can't remember what it is to see (or never were able to see in the first place) the sight-based language of the meditation may need to be changed to something more appropriate to senses you use instead, such as sound or touch.

I just can't make meditation work for me at all!

If after all of the above, meditation isn't effective, there are alternatives. Intuition is one possibility. If you've ever had a "gut reaction" to something, where you just know what's going on even though no one's told you, that's your intuition talking. Sometimes it's a warning—for example, if I go out walking one evening and I get a bad feeling about it even though I've gone out on plenty of other similar evenings, I may decide to go back inside. Other times it's a good feeling, like I just know that today I'm going to get something in the mail I've been anticipating.

In addition to guided meditation I also tend to use my intuition a lot. If I'm out hiking, for example, I may notice I feel an intuitive tug whenever I pass by a particular species of plant. When it happens, I sit down next to it and explore the feeling more deeply. Do I just think it's an especially pretty plant? Do I feel there's more to the connection? If it's the latter, I may follow it up with a guided meditation to verify; if it's secluded enough and safe to do so, I may do the meditation right there.

Note that I've personally been working with my intuition long enough that I can tell the subtle differences between when a totem wants to talk with me, versus when the individual plant spirit is interested in chatting, versus when a flower is visually appealing. There's no fast track to being able to discern these subtleties; only time and experience will help you develop these skills. Guided meditation is a way to check your work and to help you identify what you were feeling and why.

Another way people access altered states of consciousness is through active ritual. Rather than sitting quietly, they may dance, chant, sing, or recite sacred verse in order to invite totems and other beings to join them. If you have experience with rituals, try creating one that calls in the totem(s) you wish to talk to. Or you might try a grounding ritual to connect to the Earth before you do one of the exercises where you walk around outside.

If you've never done any sort of nature-based ritual before, I highly recommend Scott Cunningham's *Wicca: A Guide for the Solitary Practitioner* (Llewellyn Publications, 1989). Even if you don't consider yourself to be Wiccan, the various seasonal and lunar rituals he presents have been adapted by nature spirituality practitioners of many sorts, they're simple enough that even a beginner can give them a try, and they're a nice way to mark the changes that happen in nature throughout the year. Once you've gotten a feel for how rituals work, you can start writing your own; I recommend Elizabeth Barrette's *Composing Magic* (New Page Books, 2007) for inspiration.

Glossary

Anthropocentric: Literally "centered on man," it refers to the idea that humans are the most important species on the planet; alternately, a view of the world that places the needs and desires of humans above all else.

Biological totem: The totem of a species of living being such as an animal, plant, or fungus.

Biome: A specific type of habitat characterized by common climactic features that may be found in many places worldwide; as one example, arid deserts are found on almost all the continents of the world, though each one may have unique types of flora, fauna, and fungi living there.

Bioregion: Also known as an *ecoregion*, this is a large area of land characterized by common geographic and geological features; it will often have unique fauna, flora, and fungi not found as commonly, or at all, in adjacent bioregions.

A bioregion is frequently outlined by the watershed of a major river.

Biotope: Also known as a *habitat*, this is a more local piece of land that is defined by having a common array of fauna, flora, and fungi throughout it. These living beings are supported by its specific environmental factors, such as water, soil, and weather patterns.

Ecoregion: See *bioregion.*

Ecosystem: An ecosystem is the interconnected system of relationships among the living beings that inhabit a *biotope* and the physical features (water, soil, etc.) of the biotope.

Greenwashing: Presenting a product, service, or company as being more ecologically friendly than it actually is.

Habitat: See *biotope.*

Invasive species: A species of animal, plant, or fungus that has been introduced to a place where it is not native. This term has the additional connotation of the species being especially destructive to the ecosystem there.

Land totem: The totem of a landform or other nonbiological part of nature, such as Quartz, River, and Gravity.

Nature: Everything that exists in the physical universe. Sometimes also limited to anything that is not a human being or created by human beings, called "nonhuman nature."

Primary totem: A totem present with you for much of your life, often what people commonly think of when they say "your totem." This totem commonly has a strong influence on you to the point where other people notice you resemble it.

Secondary totem: A totem that comes into your life for a specific period of time or to help you through a particular lesson and then bows out again.

Spirituality: The art of feeling connected to something greater than yourself. What that something is may vary from person to person. Spirituality may or may not occur in the framework of an organized religion.

Tertiary totem: A totem you approach for help with a specific situation but otherwise do not share a connection.

Totem: An archetypal being that embodies all of the given qualities of a particular species or natural phenomenon; all species and natural phenomena have totems. Totems are not individual spirits; contrast an individual gray wolf spirit with the totem Gray Wolf, who watches over all gray wolves, spirits included. See also: *biological totem, land totem.*

Bibliography

Alt, David. *Glacial Lake Missoula and Its Humongous Floods.* Missoula, MT: Mountain Press Publishing Company, 2001.

Angier, Natalie. "That Cuddly Kitty is Deadlier Than You Think." Originally published 2013. Retrieved 12 May, 2014 from www.nytimes.com/2013/01/30/science/that-cuddly -kitty-of-yours-is-a-killer.html.

Catchpole, Heather. "Earliest Animals Flexed Their Muscles." Originally published 2010. Retrieved 25 October, 2013 from www.abc.net.au/science/articles/2010/02/17 /2821290.htm.

Chaney, Ralph Works. *The Ecological Significance of the Eagle Creek Flora of the Columbia River Gorge.* Originally published 1918. Retrieved 12 May, 2014 from archive.org /stream/ecologicalsignif00chan/ecologicalsignif00chan _djvu.txt.

Cline, John. "The Evolution of Sleep." Originally published 2009. Retrieved 26 October, 2013 from www.psychologytoday.com/blog/sleepless-in -america/200903/the-evolution-sleep.

"What is a Biome?" Originally published 2015. Retrieved 22 March, 2015 from eschooltoday.com/ecosystems/what-is -a-biome.html.

Hines, Sandra. "Beyond Ecological Insubordination: Speaker Urges Us to Rethink Invasive Species." Originally published 2011. Retrieved 12 May, 2014 from www.washington.edu /news/2011/10/19/beyond-ecological-insubordination -speaker-urges-us-to-rethink-invasive-species/.

Kahn, Peter, et. al. "A Plasma Display Window? The Shifting Baseline Problem in a Technologically Mediated Natural World." *Journal of Environmental Psychology* 28, no. 2 (2008): 192–199.

Kaplan, Rachel, and Stephen Kaplan. *The Experience of Nature: A Psychological Perspective.* Ann Arbor, MI: Ulrich's Bookstore, 1995.

Lerner, Rebecca. *Dandelion Hunter: Foraging the Urban Wilderness.* Guilford, CT: Lyons Press, 2013.

Louv, Richard. *The Nature Principle: Reconnecting with Life in a Virtual Age.* Chapel Hill, NC: Algonquin Books of Chapel Hill, 2012.

———. *Last Child in the Woods: Saving Our Children from Nature-Deficit Disorder.* Chapel Hill, North Carolina: Algonquin Books of Chapel Hill, 2008.

Lupa. *Plant and Fungus Totems: Connect with Spirits of Field, Forest, and Garden.* Woodbury, MN: Llewellyn Worldwide, 2014.

———. *New Paths to Animal Totems: Three Alternative Approaches to Creating Your Own Totemism.* Woodbury, MN: Llewellyn Worldwide, 2013.

Montana Natural History Center. "Glacial Lake Missoula and the Ice Age Floods." Originally published 2005. Retrieved 12 May, 2014 from http://www.glaciallakemissoula.org/.

Nelson, Richard. "Practice" In *The Sacred Earth: Writers on Nature & Spirit*, edited by Jason Gardner, 70. San Francisco: New World Library, 1998.

Olson, Miles. *The Compassionate Hunter's Guidebook: Hunting From the Heart.* Gabriola Island, Canada: New Society Publishers, 2014.

———. *Unlearn, Rewild: Earth Skills, Ideas and Inspiration for the Future Primitive.* Gabriola Island, Canada: New Society Publishers, 2014.

Roszak, Theodore. "The Nature of Sanity." Originally published 1996. Retrieved 15 October, 2013 from www.psychologytoday.com/articles/199601/the-nature-sanity.

Simon, Matt. "Fantastically Wrong: The Legend of the Homicidal Fire-Proof Salamander." Originally published 2014. Retrieved 9 March, 2015 from www.wired.com/2014/08/fantastically-wrong-homicidal-salamander.

Share, Jack. "The Ancestral Rocky Mountains and Their Eroded Remnants." Originally published 2011. Retrieved 12 May, 2014 from written-in-stone-seen-through-my-lens.blogspot.com/2011/02/ancestral-rocky-mountains-and-their.html.

Wandersee, J. H., and E. E. Schussler. "Toward a Theory of Plant Blindness." *Plant Science* bulletin 47, no. 1 (2001): 2–8.

Index

To Write the Author

If you wish to contact the author or would like more information about this book, please write to the author in care of Llewellyn Worldwide, and we will forward your request. Both the author and publisher appreciate hearing from you and learning of your enjoyment of this book and how it has helped you. Llewellyn Worldwide cannot guarantee that every letter written to the author can be answered, but all will be forwarded. Please write to:

Lupa
℅ Llewellyn Worldwide
2143 Wooddale Drive
Woodbury, MN 55125-2989

Please enclose a self-addressed stamped envelope for reply,
or $1.00 to cover costs. If outside the U.S.A., enclose
an international postal reply coupon.

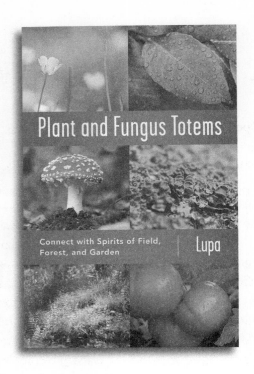

Plant and Fungus Totems

Connect with Spirits of Field, Forest, and Garden | Lupa

Plant and Fungus Totems
Connect with Spirits of Field, Forest, and Garden
LUPA

Open up to a new realm of spiritual practice. *Plant and Fungus Totems* provides techniques for creating respectful partnerships with totems, archetypal spirits that embody the qualities of their respective species. Working with just plants and fungus—or in conjunction with their animal counterparts—you will discover the wisdom these spirit beings impart to those of us who listen.

Exploring three different models of totemism, Lupa invites you to be of service to the planet's ecology by developing relationships with these often-overlooked sources of insight. Providing meditations and suggestions for journaling and experimentation, *Plant and Fungus Totems* shows how to receive guidance and helps you connect more deeply with the totemic ecosystem. Also included are hands-on exercises for incorporating physical plants and fungi into your totemic work, as well as tips for working with herbs, gardens, urban wild plants, and more.

978-0-7387-4039-3, 312 pp., 5³⁄₁₆ x 8   **$16.99**

New Paths to Animal Totems

Three Alternative Approaches
to Creating Your Own Totemism

Lupa

New Paths to Animal Totems
*Three Alternative Approaches
to Creating Your Own Totemism*
LUPA

In *New Paths to Animal Totems*, author Lupa provides a new approach to totemism that offers foundations, theories, and practices well beyond the typical pseudo-Native-American animal totem book. Exploring and blending three different models of totem work, you will create your own unique path that adds meaning and vitality to your spiritual practice. The Correspondence Model uses directions, elements, and other correspondences to create a totemic cosmology. The Bioregional Model focuses on local physical and spiritual ecosystems. In the Archetypal Model, totems represent aspects of human personality and experience.

Blending and experimenting with the three approaches provides fresh alternatives whether you are new to totemic work or are looking for a novel way to invigorate your existing practice. Hands-on rituals and meditations bring the particular strength, renewal, and wisdom that totem work creates.

978-0-7387-3337-1, 312 pp., 5³/₁₆ x 8   **$16.99**